WHICH WINE?

500 Cheese and Wine Pairings

Leonardo Linosk

2022

ABOUT THIS GUIDE

This guide is really a reference book. There are no boring rules to learn. In the Pairing Suggestions you will find American cheeses and cheeses from all over the world in alphabetical order - with some basic information about them - each one paired with two wines. You will find also tips, recipes and how to assemble boards and spreads – everything you need to know for an appetizing spread to enjoy with your friends or for yourself. I like, once in a while, to gather my friends for a night of cheese and wine tasting. I enjoy the whole process of creating a memorable night that everybody will enjoy and have fun – nothing too serious and no rules! The goal in pairing cheese and wine is to create a balance between the aroma, texture, flavor and fatness of the cheese and the aroma, weight, acidity and tannin of the wine - making it a pleasurable experience. White, Sparkling, Rosé and Red – they all have a cheese to match!

Syrah and Shiraz – they are the same grape. The spelling depends on the region and the style of the wine. Generally, Syrah is from France and Shiraz from Australia and United States.

At the end of the Pairing Suggestions there is a list of wines by country to help you when buying the wine.

If it not specified the wine is dry.

Cheese and wine are always changing due to various factors like aging, terroir, vintage and production method. The best way to learn is practicing and experimenting different pairings – that way you will find your favorite combinations. Remember that the best pairings are the ones you love the most. Have fun!

Cheers!

PAIRING SUGGESTIONS

14 Arpents
Type: Soft, cow's milk
Country of Origin: Canada (Saguenay-Lac-Saint-Jean)
Wine: Côtes-du-Rhône (white), Pinot Grigio

1924 Bleu
Type: Semi-soft, cow's and sheep's milk
Country of Origin: France (Auvergne)
Wine: Banyuls, Pineau des Charentes

A

Abbaye de Belloc
Type: Semi-hard, sheep's milk
Country of Origin: France (Aquitaine)
Wine: Blaüfrankish, Malbec

Abbaye du Mont des Cats
Type: Semi-soft, cow's milk
Country of Origin: France (Nord-Pas-de-Calais)
Wine: Graves (red), Pinot Noir

Abondance
Type: Semi-hard, cow's milk
Country of Origin: France (Haute-Savoie)
Wine: Amontillado Sherry, Pinot Gris

Acapella
Type: Soft, goat's milk
Country of Origin: Unites States (California)
Wine: Burgundy (white), Sauvignon Blanc

Adarré
Type: Firm, goat's and sheep's milk

Country of Origin: France (Loire)
Wine: Shiraz, Zinfandel

Adobera
Type: Fresh-soft, cow's milk
Country of Origin: Mexico (Los Altos de Jalisco)
Wine: Chardonnay, Sparkling Wine (white)

Afterglow
Type: Soft, goat's milk
Country of Origin: United States (Wisconsin)
Wine: Dolcetto, Vouvray

Aisy Cendré
Type: Semi-soft, cow's milk
Country of Origin: France (Burgundy)
Wine: Bordeaux (red), Burgundy (red)

Alderney
Type: Semi-soft, cow's milk
Country of Origin: Canada (Chaudière-Appalaches)
Wine: Pinot Noir, Viognier

Alisios
Type: Firm, cow's and goat's milk
Country of Origin: Spain (Canary Islands)

Wine: Malvasia (white), Provence (rosé)

Alp Blossom
Type: Semi-hard, cow's milk
Country of Origin: Germany (Bavaria)
Wine: Beaujolais, Provence (rosé)

Alpha Tolman
Type: Semi-hard, cow's milk
Country of Origin: United States (Vermont)
Wine: Pinot Noir, Riesling

Altenburger Ziegenkäse
Type: Soft, goat's milk
Country of Origin: Germany (Saxony)
Wine: Cahors (red), Sparkling Wine (rosé)

Alverca
Type: Semi-hard, goat's and sheep's milk
Country of Origin: Portugal (Alverca)
Wine: Chambourcin, Riesling

Ameribella
Type: Semi-soft, cow's milk
Country of Origin: United States (Indiana)
Wine: Cava, Gewürztraminer

Amish Blue
Type: Semi-soft, cow's milk
Country of Origin: United States (Wisconsin)
Wine: Garnacha (rosé), Zinfandel (white)

Appalachian
Type: Semi-soft, cow's milk
Country of Origin: United States (Virginia)
Wine: Chardonnay, Pinot Blanc

Appenzeller
Type: Hard, cow's milk
Country of Origin: Switzerland (Saint Gallen)
Wine: Fino Sherry, Pinot Gris

Appleby's Cheshire
Type: Hard, cow's milk
Country of Origin: United Kingdom (Shropshire)
Wine: Pinot Meunier, Syrah

Ardrahan
Type: Semi-soft, cow's milk
Country of Origin: Ireland (Duhallow)
Wine: Chenin Blanc, Pinot Noir

Aries
Type: Firm, sheep's milk
Country of Origin: United States (California)
Wine: Vinho Verde (white), Viognier

Artavaggio
Type: Soft, cow's milk
Country of Origin: Italy (Piedmont)
Wine: Pinot Noir, Sparkling Wine (white)

Ascutney Mountain
Type: Hard, cow's milk
Country of Origin: United States (Vermont)
Wine: Cabernet Sauvignon, Tempranillo

Ash Brie
Type: Soft, cow's milk
Country of Origin: Australia (Sunshine Coast)
Wine: Burgundy (white), Pinot Noir (rosé)

Asher Blue
Type: Semi-soft, cow's milk
Country of Origin: United States (Georgia)
Wine: Amarone della Valpolicella, Sauternes

Ashley
Type: Soft, cow's milk
Country of Origin: United States (Colorado)
Wine: Chardonnay, Sparkling Wine (white)

Asiago
Type: Hard, cow's milk
Country of Origin: Italy (Veneto)
Wine: Dolcetto, Merlot

Asiago Pressato
Type: Semi-soft, cow's milk
Country of Origin: Italy (Veneto)
Wine: Franciacorta, Vernaccia di San Gimignano di San Gimignano

Azeitão
Type: Semi-soft, sheep's milk
Country of Origin: Portugal (Arrabida Mountains)
Wine: Castelão, Vintage Port

B

Baby Swiss
Type: Semi-hard, cow's milk
Country of Origin: United States (Ohio)
Wine: Pinot Noir, Sauvignon Blanc

Bad Axe
Type: Semi-hard, sheep's milk
Country of Origin: United States (Wisconsin)
Wine: Madiran (red), Palo Cortado Sherry

Balsamic Bellavitano
Type: Hard, cow's milk
Country of Origin: United States (Wisconsin)
Wine: Pinot Noir, Sparkling Wine (white)

Banon
Type: Soft, goat's milk
Country of Origin: France (Banon and Provence)
Wine: Chenin Blanc, Provence (Rosé)

Bassigny au Porto
Type: Semi-soft, cow's milk

Country of Origin: France (Burgundy)
Wine: Banyuls, Tawny Port

Batzos
Type: Semi-hard, goat's or sheep's milk
Country of Origin: Greece (Thessaly, Western and Central Macedonia)
Wine: Sparkling Wine (white), Xinomavro

Bayley Hazen Blue
Type: Semi-hard, cow's milk
Country of Origin: United States (Vermont)
Wine: Pinot Noir, Tawny Port

Bear Hill
Type: Semi-hard, sheep's milk
Country: United States (Vermont)
Wine: Grüner Veltliner, Riesling

Beaufort
Type: Hard, cow's milk
Country of Origin: France (Haute-Savoie)
Wine: Chardonnay, Seyssel (white)

Beenleigh Blue
Type: Soft, sheep's milk

Country of Origin: England (Devon)
Wine: Icewine, Monbazillac

Bel Ceillo

Type: Semi-hard, cow's milk
Country of Origin: United States (New York)
Wine: Cabernet Sauvignon, Syrah

Bellavitano Gold

Type: Hard, cow's milk
Country of Origin: United States (Wisconsin)
Wine: Dolcetto d'Alba, Pinot Nero

Belle-Mère

Type: Semi-soft, cow's milk
Country of Origin: Canada (Saguenay-Lac-Saint-Jean)
Wine: Müller-Thurgau, Riesling

Bel Paese

Type: Semi-soft, cow's milk
Country of Origin: Italy (Lombardy)
Wine: Barbera, Pinot Noir

Bergader Cremosissimo

Type: Soft, cow's milk
Country of Origin: Germany (Bavaria)

Wine: Beaujolais, Sparkling Wine (white)

Berkswell

Type: Hard, sheep's milk
Country of Origin: United Kingdom (West Midlands)
Wine: Chianti, Tempranillo

Bermuda Triangle

Type: Semi-soft, cow's milk
Country of Origin: United States (California)
Wine: Pinot Noir (rosé), Sauvignon Blanc

Big Holmes

Type: Firm, sheep's milk
Country of Origin: United States (Wisconsin)
Wine: Sparkling Wine (rosé), Zinfandel

Big Woods

Type: Semi-hard, sheep's milk
Country of Origin: United States (Minnesota)
Wine: Icewine, Riesling (off-dry)

Black Pearl

Type: Semi-hard, goat's milk
Country of Origin: Australia (Mornington Peninsula)
Wine: Gamay, Provence (rosé)

Blacksticks Blue
Type: Soft, cow's milk
Country of Origin: England (Lancashire)
Wine: Tokaji, Zinfandel

Black Truffle Cheddar
Type: Firm, cow's milk
Country of Origin: United States (Vermont)
Wine: Madiran (red), Merlot

Bleu d'Auvergne
Type: Semi-soft (blue), cow's milk
Country of Origin: France (Auvergne)
Wine: Monbazillac, Sauternes

Blu del Moncenisio
Type: Semi-soft (blue), cow's milk
Country of Origin: Italy (Moncenisio Pass)
Wine: Gewürztraminer, Sauternes

Bocconcini
Type: Semi-soft, cow's and water buffalo's milk
Country of Origin: Italy (Campania)
Wine: Sauvignon Blanc, Sparkling Wine (white)

Boerenkaas
Type: Semi-hard, cow's, goat's or sheep's milk
Country of Origin: Netherlands (Overijssel)
Wine: Amontillado Sherry, Sparkling Wine (white)

Bon Anniversaire
Type: Semi-soft, cow's milk
Country of Origin: United States (Massachusetts)
Wine: Cava, Vernacchia di San Gimignano

Bonne Bouche
Type: Soft, goat's milk
Country of Origin: United States (Vermont)
Wine: Burgundy (red), Sancerre

Boschetto al Tartufo
Type: Semi-soft, cow's and sheep's milk
Country of Origin: Italy (Tuscany)
Wine: Barolo, Barbaresco

Boursault
Type: Soft, cow's milk
Country of Origin: France (Val-de-Marne)
Wine: Chablis, Vouvray

Boursin
Type: Soft, cow's milk
Country of Origin: France (Croisy-sur-Eure)
Wine: Pinot Noir, Sparkling Wine (white)

Bra Duro
Type: Hard, cow's milk
Country of Origin: Italy (Piedmont)
Wine: Cabernet Sauvignon, Nebbiolo

Brebirousse d'Argental
Type: Soft, sheep's milk
Country of Origin: France (Loire)
Wine: Champagne, Loire (rosé)

Brebis
Type: Semi-hard, sheep's milk
Country of Origin: France (Aquitaine)
Wine: Pessac-Léognan (white), Sparkling Wine (white)

Bresse Bleu
Type: Soft (blue), cow's milk
Country of Origin: France (Burgundy)
Wine: Chablis, Sauternes

Brick
Type: Semi-soft, cow's milk
Country of Origin: United States (Wisconsin)
Wine: Merlot, Pinot Noir

Bridgewater
Type: Soft, cow's milk
Country of Origin: United States (Michigan)
Wine: Riesling, Schiava

Bridgid's Abbey
Type: Semi-soft, cow's milk
Country of Origin: United States (Connecticut)
Wine: Côtes de Nuit (red), Garnacha

Brie
Type: Soft, cow's milk
Country of Origin: France (Seine-et-Marne)
Wine: Burgundy (red), Chardonnay

Brillat-Savarin
Type: Soft, cow's milk
Country of Origin: France (Ile de France)
Wine: Sparkling Wine (rosé), Viognier

Brin d'Amour
Type: Semi-soft, sheep's milk
Country of Origin: France (Corsica)
Wine: Sauvignon Blanc, Vermentino

Bru-XL
Type: Firm, cow's milk
Country of Origin: Belgium
Wine: Bordeaux (red), Shiraz

Bucherondin
Type: Semi-firm, goat's milk
Country of Origin: France (Loire)
Wine: Crémant de Loire, Sauvignon Blanc

Bufaletto
Type: Soft, buffalo's and cow's milk
Country of Origin: Italy (Lombardy)
Wine: Greco di Tufo, Fiano di Avellino

Buncom in Bloom
Type: Soft, cow's milk
Country of Origin: United States (Oregon)
Wine: Chardonnay (oaked), Pinot Noir

Butterbloom
Type: Soft, cow's milk
Country of Origin: United States (Oregon)
Wine: Provence (rosé), Sparkling Wine (white)

Buttermilk Blue
Type: Semi-hard, cow's milk
Country of Origin: United States (Wisconsin)
Wine: Banyuls, Pineau des Charentes (white)

Burrata
Type: Fresh-Soft, water buffalo's milk
Country of Origin: Italy (Apulia)
Wine: Fiano di Avellino, Roero Arneis

C

Caboc
Type: Soft, cow's milk
Country of Origin: Scotland (Tain)
Wine: Beaujolais, Pinot Gris

Cabra al Romero
Type: Firm, goat's milk
Country of Origin: Spain (Murcia)
Wine: Albariño, Syrah

Cabra LaMancha
Type: Semi-soft, goat's milk
Country of Origin: United States (Maryland)
Wine: Pinot Noir, Sauvignon Blanc

Cabrales
Type: Soft, cow's, goat's and sheep's milk
Country of Origin: Spain (Asturias)
Wine: Sauternes, Tawny Port

Cabra Transmontano
Type: Soft, goat's milk

Country of Origin: Portugal (Alto Douro)
Wine: Alvarinho, Tawny Port

Caciocavallo
Type: Fresh-soft, cow's milk
Country of Origin: Italy (Basilicata)
Wine: Aglianico, Vernaccia di San Gimignano di San Gimignano

Caciotta di Capra Foglie di Noce
Type: Semi-hard, goat's milk
Country of Origin: Italy (Bagnolo di San Pietro di Feletto)
Wine: Albariño, Sauvignon Blanc

Cachalot
Type: Hard, cow's milk
Country of Origin: United States (Connecticut)
Wine: Bordeaux (red), Merlot

Caerphilly
Type: Hard, cow's milk
Country of Origin: United Kingdom (Wales)
Wine: Burgundy (white), Champagne

Calderwood
Type: Firm, cow's milk
Country of Origin: United States (Vermont)
Wine: Chardonnay (oaked), Gewürztraminer

Callisto
Type: Semi-firm, cow's milk
Country of Origin: United States (Oregon)
Wine: Pinot Blanc, Pinot Noir

Calvander
Type: Firm, cow's milk
Country of Origin: United States (North Carolina)
Wine: Cabernet Sauvignon, Merlot

Cambozola Grand Noir
Type: Semi-soft (blue), cow's milk
Country of Origin: Germany (Allgäu)
Wine: Chardonnay, Moscato d'Asti

Camembert
Type: Soft, cow's milk
Country of Origin: France (Normandy)
Wine: Chenin Blanc, Sparkling Wine (white)

Campo
Type: Semi-soft, cow's milk
Country of Origin: United States (North Carolina)
Wine: Cabernet Franc, Nebbiolo

Canastra
Type: Soft, cow's milk
Country of Origin: Brazil (Minas Gerais)
Wine: Tawny Port, Vinho Verde (white)

Cancoillotte
Type: Soft, cow's milk
Country of Origin: France (Franche-Comté)
Wine: Arbois (white), Vinho Verde (white)

Canela
Type: Hard, cow's milk
Country of Origin: United States (Wisconsin)
Wine: La Mancha (red), Sercial Madeira

Cantal
Type: Soft, cow's milk
Country of Origin: France (Cantal)
Wine: Beaujolais, Pinot Gris

Capriella
Type: Soft, cows' and goat's milk
Country of Origin: United States (Texas)
Wine: Sauvignon Blanc, Sémillon

Carmody
Type: Firm, cow's milk
Country of Origin: United States (California)
Wine: Merlot, Pinot Noir

Carnia
Type: Hard, cow's milk
Country of Origin: Italy (Carnia)
Wine: Bardolino, Beaujolais

Cashel Blue
Type: Soft, sheep's milk
Country of Origin: Ireland (County Tipperary)
Wine: Sauternes, Vin Santo

Castelmagno
Type: Semi-hard, cow's, goat's and sheep's milk
Country of Origin: Italy (Piedmont)
Wine: Barolo, Nebbiolo

Castel Rosso
Type: Semi-hard, cow's milk
Country of Origin: Italy (Piedmont)
Wine: Beaujolais Village, Nebbiolo

Cave Aged Marisa
Type: Semi-hard, sheep's milk
Country of Origin: United States (Wisconsin)
Wine: Gamay, Pinot Noir

Caveman Blue
Type: Semi-hard, cow's milk
Country of Origin: United States (Oregon)
Wine: Tokaji, Zinfandel

Chabichou du Poitou
Type: Semi-soft, goat's milk
Country of Origin: France (Poitou-Charentes)
Wine: Chardonnay, Sancerre

Challerhocker
Type: Hard, cow's milk
Country of Origin: Switzerland (St. Gallen)
Wine: Chardonnay, Pinot Noir

Champayeur

Type: Soft, cow's milk
Country of Origin: Canada (Centre-du-Québec)
Wine: Albariño, Gewürztraminer

Chanco

Type: Semi-hard, cow's milk
Country of Origin: Chile (Maule)
Wine: Chardonnay, Sparkling Wine (white)

Chaource

Type: Soft, cow's milk
Country of Origin: France (Aube)
Wine: Burgundy (white), Sparkling Wine (white)

Chaumes

Type: Soft, cow's milk
Country of Origin: France (St. Antoine)
Wine: Bourdeaux (red), Valpolicella

Cheddar

Type: Hard, cow's milk
Country of Origin: England (Somerset)
Wine: Cabernet Sauvignon, Merlot

Cheddar, Irish Extra-Sharp
Type: Firm, cow's milk
Country of Origin: Ireland (County Cork)
Wine: Cabernet Sauvignon, Sparkling Wine (Rosé)

Chèvre
Type: Soft, goat's milk
Country of Origin: France (Central Regions)
Wine: Sauvignon Blanc, Sparkling Wine (white)

Chevrotin des Aravis
Type: Semi-hard, goat's milk
Country of Origin: France (Haute-Savoie)
Wine: Chasselas, Sparkling Wine (white)

Chimay Trappist Beer Washed
Type: Semi-soft, cow's milk
Country of Origin: Belgium (Chimay)
Wine: Chenin Blanc, Sparkling Wine (white)

Chiriboga Blue
Type: Semi-soft, cow's milk
Country of Origin: Germany (Allgäu)
Wine: Gave, Riesling

Chocolate Lab
Type: Hard, cow's milk
Country of Origin: United States (North Carolina)
Wine: Malbec, Sparkling Wine (rosé)

Chorherrenkase
Type: Semi-firm, cow's milk
Country of Origin: Austria (Tirol)
Wine: Rioja (white), Saint-Chinian (red)

Ciao Angelo
Type: Hard, cow's milk
Country of Origin: Netherlands (Holland)
Wine: Bordeaux (red), Cabernet Franc

Clisson
Type: Firm, goat's milk
Country of Origin: France (Bordeaux)
Wine: Muscadet, Pinot Gris

Clochette
Type: Hard, goat's milk
Country of Origin: France (Poitou-Charantes)
Wine: Pinot Grigio, Pinot Noir

Cocoa Cardona
Type: Firm, goat's milk
Country of Origin: United States (Wisconsin)
Wine: Gewürztraminer, Syrah

ColoRouge
Type: Soft, cow's milk
Country of Origin: United States (Colorado)
Wine: Beaujolais, Chardonnay

Comté
Type: Semi-hard, cow's milk
Country of Origin: France (Massif du Jura)
Wine: Palo Cortado Sherry, Pinot Gris

Cooleeney
Type: Soft, cow's milk
Country of Origin: Ireland (Tipperary)
Wine: Pinot Noir, Sparkling Wine (white)

Coppinger
Type: Semi-soft, cow's milk
Country of Origin: United States (Tennessee)
Wine: Barbera, Gewürztraminer

Cornish Yarg
Type: Semi-hard, cow's milk
Country of Origin: England (Cornwall)
Wine: Chardonnay, Sparkling Wine (white)

Cotija
Type: Fresh-firm, cow's milk
Country of Origin: Mexico (Michoacán and Jalisco)
Wine: Cabernet Sauvignon, Mezcal

Cotswold
Type: Semi-hard, cow's milk
Country of Origin: England (Gloucestershire County)
Wine: Shiraz, Zinfandel

Cottonbell
Type: Soft, cow's milk
Country of Origin: United States (North Carolina)
Wine: Chardonnay, Roero Arneis

Coulommiers
Type: Soft, cow's milk
Country of Origin: France (Seine-et-Marne)
Wine: Pinot Grigio, Sauternes

Coupole

Type: Soft, goat's milk
Country of Origin: United States (Vermont)
Wine: Côtes-du-Rhône (white), Riesling

Cream Cheese

Type: Soft-fresh, cow's milk
Country of Origin: United States (New York)
Wine: Chardonnay, Pinot Noir

Cremont

Type: Soft, cow's and goat's milk
Country of Origin: United States (Vermont)
Wine: Sauvignon Blanc, Vinho Verde (white)

Crescenza

Type: Soft-fresh, cow's milk
Country of Origin: Italy (Lombardy, Piedmont, and Veneto)
Wine: Chardonnay, Viognier

Crottin de Chavignol

Type: Hard, goat's milk
Country of Origin: France (Loire)
Wine: Côtes-du-Rhône (white), Sauvignon Blanc

Crowdie
Type: Soft-fresh, cow's milk
Country of Origin: Scotland (Tain)
Wine: Riesling, Sauvignon Blanc

Crowley
Type: Semi-soft, cow's milk
Country of Origin: United States (Vermont)
Wine: Cabernet Sauvignon, Malbec

Crozier
Type: Semi-soft (blue), sheep's milk
Country of Origin: Ireland (Tipperary)
Wine: Late Harvest Chenin Blanc, Zinfandel

Crucolo
Type: Semi-soft, cow's milk
Country of Origin: Italy (Trentino)
Wine: Barbera d'Alba, Chardonnay

Curworthy
Type: Semi-hard, cow's milk
Country of Origin: England (Devon)
Wine: Pinot Noir (rosé), Sparkling Wine (rosé)

D

Dalmatinac
Type: Semi-firm, cow's and sheep's milk
Country of Origin: Croatia (Pag Island)
Wine: Franciacorta, Sauvignon Blanc

Damona
Type: Semi-soft, cow's milk
Country of Origin: United States (Oregon)
Wine: Sauvignon Blanc, Sekt

Danablu
Type: Soft, cow's milk
Country of Origin: Denmark (Viby)
Wine: Amarone della Valpolicella, Gewürztraminer

Delft Blue
Type: Soft, cow's milk
Country of Origin: Netherlands (Delft)
Wine: Malbec, Moscato d'Asti

Délice de Bourgogne
Type: Soft, cow's milk

Country of Origin: France (Burgundy)
Wine: Burgundy (red), Chardonnay

Devil's Gulch
Type: Semi-soft, cow's milk
Country of Origin: United States (California)
Wine: Icewine, Moscato

Dilly Girl
Type: Semi-hard, cow's milk
Country of Origin: United States (New York)
Wine: Crémant de Loire (rosé), Shiraz

Dirt Lover
Type: Semi-soft, sheep's milk
Country of Origin: United States (Missouri)
Wine: Grenache (rosé), Sauvignon Blanc

Dolcelatte
Type: Blue-soft, cow's milk
Country of Origin: Italy (Lombardy)
Wine: Amarone della Valpolicella, Tawny Port

Dorset Mini
Type: Semi-soft, cow's milk
Country of Origin: United States (Vermont)

Wine: Crozes-Hermitage (white) Sparkling Wine (rosé)

Dorstone
Type: Soft, goat's milk
Country of Origin: England (Herefordshire)
Wine: Muscadet, Sparkling Wine (white)

Douce Moitié
Type: Firm, cow's and goat's milk
Country of Origin: Canada (Laval)
Wine: Gewürztraminer, Riesling

Drunken Goat
Type: Semi-soft, goat's milk
Country of Origin: Spain (Murcia)
Wine: Monastrell, Murcia (red)

Dubliner
Type: Hard, cow's milk
Country of Origin: Ireland (County Cork)
Wine: Chardonnay (oaked), Cabernet Sauvignon

Durrus
Type: Semi-soft, cow's milk
Country of Origin: Ireland (West Cork)
Wine: Gewürztraminer, Pinot Gris

Dutchman's Peak

Type: Semi-soft, cow's milk
Country of Origin: United States (Oregon)
Wine: Gamay, Pinot Noir

E

Edam
Type: Semi-hard, cow's or goat's milk
Country of Origin: Netherlands
Wine: Burgundy (red), Syraz

Edelpilz
Type: Soft, cow's milk
Country of Origin: Germany (Bavaria)
Wine: Pinot Gris, Sylvaner Spätlese

Eidolon
Type: Semi-soft, cow's milk
Country of Origin: United States (Massachusetts)
Wine: Provence (rosé), Sparkling Wine (rosé)

Elk Mountain
Type: Hard, goat's milk
Country of Origin: United States (Oregon)
Wine: Sparkling Wine (rosé), Shiraz

El Piconero al Cognac
Type: Firm, sheep's milk

Country of Origin: Spain (La Mancha)
Wine: Airén, Cognac

Emmental
Type: Hard, cow's milk
Country of Origin: Switzerland (Bern)
Wine: Riesling, Syrah

Époisses
Type: Soft, cow's milk
Country of Origin: France (Burgundy)
Wine: Burgundy (red), Gewürztraminer

Espresso Bellavitanno
Type: Semi-firm, cow's milk
Country of Origin: United States (Wisconsin)
Wine: Pinot Noir, Shiraz

Esrom
Type: Semi-soft, cow's milk
Country of Origin: Denmark (Århus)
Wine: Burgundy (red), Cava

Estepe
Type: Semi-hard, cow's milk
Country of Origin: Brazil (Minas Gerais)

Wine: Sauvignon Blanc, Sparkling Wine (white)

Etivaz
Type: Firm, cow's milk
Country of Origin: Switzerland (Vaud)
Wine: Gamay, Minervois (red)

Etorki
Type: Hard, sheep's milk
Country of Origin: France (Pyrénées-Atlantiques)
Wine: Côtes-du-Rhône (white), Sparkling Wine (white)

Explorateur
Type: Soft, cow's milk
Country of Origin: France (Seine-et-Marne)
Wine: Faugères (white), Prosecco (rosé)

Ewenique
Type: Firm, sheep's milk
Country of Origin: United States (California)
Wine: Grenache (rosé), Sparkling Wine (rosé)

F

Fat Bottom Girl
Type: Semi-hard, sheep's milk
Country of Origin: United States (California)
Wine: Grenache (red), Zweigelt

Feta
Type: Soft, sheep's milk
Country of Origin: Greece (Macedonia)
Wine: Assyrtico, Pinot Gris

Figueira
Type: Semi-hard, cow's milk
Country of Origin: Brazil (São Paulo)
Wine: Malbec (rosé), Sauvignon Blanc

Fior d'Arancio
Type: Soft (blue), cow's milk
Country of Origin: Italy (Veneto)
Wine: Fior d'Arancio (sweet), Moscato d'Asti

Fior di Latte
Type: Semi-soft, cow's milk

Country of Origin: Australia (New South Wales)
Wine: Bardolino, Lambrusco di Sobarba

Fiore Sardo
Type: Semi-hard, sheep's milk
Country of Origin: Italy (Sardinia)
Wine: Cannonau, Monica di Sardegna

Five Counties
Type: Semi-firm, cow's milk
Country of Origin: England (Somerset)
Wine: Bordeaux (red), Cabernet Sauvignon

Florette
Type: Soft, goat's milk
Country of Origin: France (Rhône-Alps)
Wine: Crémant d'Alsace, Grüner Veltliner

Fontina
Type: Semi-hard, cow's milk
Country of Origin: Italy (Aosta Valley)
Wine: Pinot Noir, Viognier

Formagella
Type: Semi-soft, cow's milk
Country of Origin: United States (California)

Wine: Chablis, Vouvray

Fougerus
Type: Soft, cow's milk
Country of Origin: France (Seine-et-Marne)
Wine: Burgundy (red), Crémant d'Alsace

Fourmage
Type: Semi-hard, buffalo's, cow's, goat's and sheep's milk
Country of Origin: Netherlands (Holland)
Wine: Cava, Prosecco

Fourme d'Ambert
Type: Soft, cow's milk
Country of Origin: France (Auvergne)
Wine: Pinot Noir, Syrah

Frère Chasseur
Type: Firm, cow's milk
Country of Origin: Canada (Montérégie)
Wine: Carignan, Grenache (red)

Fromage Blanc
Type: Soft-fresh, cow's milk
Country of Origin: France (Normandy)

Wine: Grechetto, Sauvignon Blanc

Fromage de Meaux
Type: Soft, cow's milk
Country of Origin: France (Île de France)
Wine: Gamay, Merlot

G

Gabietou
Type: Semi-soft, cow's and sheep's milk
Country of Origin: France (Pau)
Wine: Beaujolais (white), Riesling

Garrotxa
Type: Semi-firm, goat's milk
Country of Origin: Spain (Catalonia)
Wine: Albariño, Pinot Gris

Gédéon
Type: Firm, cow's milk
Country of Origin: Canada (Saguenay-Lac-Saint-Jean)
Wine: Gamay, Pinot Noir

Geit in Stad
Type: Firm, goat's milk
Country of Origin: United States (California)
Wine: Cabernet Franc, Sparkling Wine (white)

Giramundo
Type: Semi-hard, cow's milk

Country of Origin: Brazil (São Paulo)
Wine: Chardonnay, Sparkling Wine (white)

Gjetost
Type: Semi-hard, cow's and goat's milk
Country of Origin: Norway (Gudbrand Valley)
Wine: Aquavit, Oloroso Sherry

Glacier Wildfire Blue
Type: Semi-soft, cow's milk
Country of Origin: United States (Wisconsin)
Wine: LBV Port, Reciotto della Valpolicella

Good Thunder
Type: Semi-hard, cow's milk
Country of Origin: United States (Minnesota)
Wine: Chenin Blanc, Gewürztraminer

Gorgonzola
Type: Soft-Blue, cow's milk
Country of Origin: Italy (Piedmont and Lombardy)
Wine: Amarone della Valpolicella, Banyuls

Gorgonzola Dolce
Type: Soft, cow's milk
Country of Origin: Italy (Bergamo and Cremona)

Wine: Sparkling Wine (white), Vin Santo

Gorgonzola Piccante
Type: Soft, cow's milk
Country of Origin: Italy (Lombardy)
Wine: Sauternes, Viognier

Gouda
Type: Semi-hard, cow's milk
Country of Origin: Netherlands (South Holland)
Wine: Chardonnay, Sparkline Wine (white)

Gouda, Aged
Type: Hard, cow's, goat's or sheep's milk
Country of Origin: Holland (Gouda)
Wine: Amarone della Valpolicella, Barbaresco

Gouda, Goat
Type: Semi-firm, goat's milk
Country of Origin: United States (California)
Wine: Pouilly-Fumé, Sauvignon Blanc

Gouda, Green Pesto
Type: Firm, cow's milk
Country of Origin: Netherlands (Holland)
Wine: Pinot Grigio, Trebbiano

Gouda, Guacamole
Type: Semi-hard, cow's milk
Country of Origin: Netherlands (Holland)
Wine: Sauvignon Blanc, Torrontés

Graddost
Type: Semi-hard, cow's milk
Country of Origin: Scandinavia (Sweden)
Wine: Chenin Blanc, Sauvignon Blanc

Grana Padano DOP
Type: Hard, cow's milk
Country of Origin: Italy (Po River Valley)
Wine: Greco di Tufo, Prosecco

Grana Padano 16 Months
Type: Hard, cow's milk
Country of Origin: Italy (Po River Valley)
Wine: Montepulciano d'Abruzzo, Primitivo

Grana Padano Reserve
Type: Hard, cow's milk
Country of Origin: Italy (Po River Valley)
Wine: Amarone della Valpolicella, Brunello di Montalcino

Grand Cru Gruyère Surchoix
Type: Semi-hard, cow's milk
Country of Origin: United States (Wisconsin)
Wine: Chardonnay, Riesling

Gran Kinara
Type: Hard, cow's milk
Country of Origin: Italy (Piedmont)
Wine: Barbaresco, Prosecco

Grassias
Type: Soft, cow's and goat's milk
Country of Origin: United States (Texas)
Wine: Sauvignon Blanc, Sparkling Wine (white)

Graviéra Kritis
Type: Hard, cow's, goat's and sheep's milk
Country of Origin: Greece (Crete, Lesbos, Naxos and Amfilochia)
Wine: Robola, Vidiano

Grayson
Type: Semi-soft, cow's milk
Country of Origin: United States (Virginia)
Wine: Chardonnay, Riesling

Green Hill

Type: Soft, cow's milk
Country of Origin: United States (Georgia)
Wine: Pinot Noir, Sémillon

Grevé

Type: Semi-hard, cow's milk
Country of Origin: Sweden (Örnsköldsvik)
Wine: Gewürztraminer, Roero Arneis

Grey Owl

Type: Semi-soft, goat's milk
Country of Origin: Canada (Québec)
Wine: Riesling, Sauvignon Blanc

Griffin

Type: Firm, cow's milk
Country of Origin: United States (Georgia)
Wine: Chardonnay, Pinot Grigio

Grinzing

Type: Semi-soft, cow's milk
Country of Origin: Austria (Grinzing)
Wine: Riesling, Grenache (red)

Gruyère
Type: Hard, cow's milk
Country of Origin: Switzerland (Fribourg)
Wine: Pinot Gris, Prosecco

Gubbeen
Type: Semi-soft, cow's milk
Country of Origin: Ireland (County Cork)
Wine: Gewürztraminer, Riesling

H

Habanero Cheddar
Type: Semi-hard, cow's milk
Country of Origin: United States (Oregon)
Wine: Manzanilla Sherry, Vinho Verde (white)

Halleck Creek
Type: Semi-soft, cow's milk
Country of Origin: United States (California)
Wine: Beaujolais, Grüner Veltliner

Halloumi
Type: Semi-soft, cow's, goat's and sheep's milk
Country of Origin: Middle East (Cyprus)
Wine: Pinot Gris, Sauvignon Blanc

Hannah
Type: Semi-hard, cow's and sheep's milk
Country of Origin: United States (Oregon)
Wine: Corbières (red), Rioja (white)

Harbison
Type: Soft, cow's milk

Country of Origin: United States (Vermont)
Wine: Gamay, Roero Arneis

Harlech
Type: Semi-soft, cow's milk
Country of Origin: United Kingdom (Gwent)
Wine: Burgundy (red), Sparkling Wine (white)

Harvest Moon
Type: Hard, cow's milk
Country of Origin: United States (New York)
Wine: Aglianico, Rioja (red)

Haut-Marais de l'isle
Type: Firm, cow's milk
Country of Origin: Canada (Chaudière-Appalaches)
Wine: Cabernet Franc, Garnacha

Havarti
Type: Semi-soft, cow's milk
Country of Origin: Denmark (Vejle)
Wine: Chardonnay, Franciacorta

Havilah
Type: Hard, cow's milk
Country of Origin: United States (New Jersey)

Wine: Aglianico, Franciacorta

Haystack Peak
Type: Soft, goat's milk
Country of Origin: United States (Colorado)
Wine: Gewürztraminer, Sancerre

Heidi
Type: Firm, cow's milk
Country of Origin: Canada (British Columbia)
Wine: Chardonnay, Pinot Noir

Herbs de Humboldt
Type: Soft-fresh, goat's milk
Country of Origin: United States (California)
Wine: Cabernet Franc (Loire), Muscadet

Hereford Hop
Type: Semi-hard, cow's milk
Country of Origin: England (Gloucestershire)
Wine: Chardonnay, Sauvignon Blanc

Herrgardsost
Type: Semi-hard, cow's milk
Country of Origin: Sweden (Vadenost)
Wine: Merlot, Sparkling Wine (white)

Hoch Ybrig
Type: Firm, cow's milk
Country of Origin: Switzerland (Küssnacht)
Wine: Riesling, Zinfandel (white)

Hoja Santa
Type: Soft, goat's milk
Country of Origin: United States (Texas)
Wine: Sauvignon Blanc, Sparkling Wine (white)

Hooligan
Type: Soft, cow's milk
Country of Origin: United States (Connecticut)
Wine: Franciacorta, Poulsard

Hopyard Cheddar
Type: Semi-hard, cow's milk
Country of Origin: United States (Oregon)
Wine: Riesling, Sparkling Wine (white)

Humble
Type: Semi-soft, cow's milk
Country of Origin: United States (Vermont)
Wine: Riesling, Roero Arneis

Humboldt Fog
Type: Soft, goat's milk
Country of Origin: United States (California)
Wine: Chenin Blanc, Sancerre

I

Iberico
Type: Firm, cow's, goat's and sheep's milk
Country of Origin: Spain (Castile-La Mancha)
Wine: Airén, Cava

Ibores
Type: Firm, goat's milk
Country of Origin: Spain (Extremadura)
Wine: Cava, Ribera del Guadiana (white)

Idaho Goatster
Type: Hard, goat's milk
Country of Origin: United States (Idaho)
Wine: Gamay, Merlot

Idiazábal
Type: Hard, sheep's milk
Country of Origin: Spain (Basque and Navarra)
Wine: Priorat (red), Ribera del Duero (red)

Idyll Gris
Type: Soft, goat's milk

Country of Origin: United States (Michigan)
Wine: Chenin Blanc, Prosecco

Innes Log
Type: Soft, goat's cheese
Country of Origin: England (Staffordshire)
Wine: Bordeaux (white), Sauvignon Blanc

Iris
Type: Firm, goat's milk
Country of Origin: United States (Oregon)
Wine: Riesling, Sauvignon Blanc

Isle of Mull
Type: Hard, cow's milk
Country of Origin: Scotland (Inner Hebrides)
Wine: Merlot, Rondo

Italico
Type: Semi-hard, cow's milk
Country of Origin: United States (Wisconsin)
Wine: Valpolicella Ripasso, Vin Santo

J

Jalapeno Cheddar
Type: Semi-hard, cow's milk
Country of Origin: United States (Oregon)
Wine: Gewürztraminer, Riesling (off-dry)

Jarlsberg
Type: Semi-hard, cow's milk
Country of Origin: Norway (Jarlsberg)
Wine: Gewürztraminer, Merlot

Jeune Autize
Type: Semi-soft, goat's milk
Country of Origin: France (Loire)
Wine: Anjou (white), Sancerre

Jeune-Coeur
Type: Soft, cow's milk
Country of Origin: Canada (Gaspésie-Îles-de-la-Madaleine)
Wine: Gewürztraminer, Müller-Thurgau

Jùscht
Type: Semi-soft, cow's milk
Country of Origin: Switzerland (Gantrisch)
Wine: Chardonnay, Pinot Gris

K

Kanaal
Type: Semi-firm, cow's milk
Country of Origin: Netherlands (Overijssel)
Wine: Riesling, Sercial Madeira

Kashar
Type: Hard, cow's milk
Country of Origin: United States (Vermont)
Wine: Cava, Gewürztraminer

Kasseri
Type: Semi-hard, goat's and sheep's milk
Country of Origin: Greece (Thessaly, Macedonia, Lesbos, or Xanthi)
Wine: Agiorgitiko, Roditis

Kénogami
Type: Soft, cow's milk
Country of Origin: Canada (Saguenay-Lac-Sainte-Jean)
Wine: Chenin Blanc (off-dry), Riesling (off-dry)

Kokos Coconut
Type: Firm, cow's milk
Country of Origin: United States (Washington)
Wine: Chardonnay (oaked), Rioja (white)

Kugelkase
Type: Soft, cow's milk
Country of Origin: Austria (Danube)
Wine: Gewürztraminer, Riesling

Kunik
Type: Soft, cow's and goat's milk
Country of Origin: United States (New York)
Wine: Pinot Noir, Sparkling Wine (rosé)

L

La Di Da Lavender Cheddar
Type: Semi-hard, cow's milk
Country of Origin: United States (Oregon)
Wine: Prosecco (rosé), Provence (rosé)

Lagrein
Type: Firm, cow's milk
Country of Origin: Italy (Alto Adige)
Wine: Lagrein (red), Prosecco

Laguiole
Type: Semi-hard, cow's milk
Country of Origin: France (Aveyron)
Wine: Gamay, Sparkling Wine (rosé)

La Serena
Type: Soft, sheep's milk
Country of Origin: Spain (Extremadura)
Wine: Rioja Joven (red), Tempranillo

Lamb Chopper
Type: Hard, sheep's milk

Country of Origin: United States (California)
Wine: Burgundy (red), Vouvray

Lancashire

Type: Soft-fresh, cow's milk
Country of Origin: England (Lancashire)
Wine: Muscadet, Sparkling Wine (white)

La Peral

Type: Semi-soft (blue), cow's milk
Country of Origin: Spain (Asturias)
Wine: Oloroso Sherry, Tempranillo

L'Édel de Cléron

Type: Soft, cow's milk
Country of Origin: France (Franche-Comté)
Wine: Pinot Gris, Riesling

Leicestershire

Type: Hard, Cow's Milk
Country of Origin: England (Leicestershire)
Wine: Sauvignon Blanc, Vouvray

Leonora

Type: Semi-soft, goat's milk
Country of Origin: Spain (Castilla Leon)

Wine: Albariño, Cava

L'Etivaz
Type: Firm, cow's milk
Country of Origin: Switzerland (Vaud Alps)
Wine: Gamay, Soave

Le Wavreumont
Type: Semi-soft, cow's milk
Country of Origin: Belgium (Wallonia)
Wine: Entre-Deux-Mers, Müller-Thurgau

Leyden
Type: Hard, cow's milk
Country of Origin: Netherlands (Leyden)
Wine: Grenache (red), Shiraz

Limburger
Type: Semi-soft, cow's milk
Country of Origin: Belgium (Duchy of Limburg)
Wine: Gewürztraminer, Riesling Auslese

Lincolnshire Poacher
Type: Hard, cow's milk
Country of Origin: England (Lincolnshire)
Wine: Burgundy (white), Rioja (red)

Lindsay
Type: Firm, goat's milk
Country of Origin: Canada (Ontario)
Wine: Chardonnay, Muscadet

Lissome
Type: Soft, cow's milk
Country of Origin: United States (North Carolina)
Wine: Bonarda, Lambrusco (red)

Little Hosner
Type: Soft, cow's milk
Country of Origin: United States (Vermont)
Wine: Nebiollo, Prosecco (rosé)

Livarot
Type: Soft, cow's milk
Country of Origin: France (Normandy)
Wine: Pinot Gris, Pomerol (red)

Louis Cyr
Type: Firm, cow's milk
Country of Origin: Canada (Québec)
Wine: Chablis, Pinot Gris

Lune de Miel
Type: Semi-soft, cow's milk
Country of Origin: Canada (Bas-Saint-Laurent)
Wine: Bobal, Grenache (red)

M

Madelaine
Type: Soft, sheep's milk
Country of Origin: Canada (Eastern Townships)
Wine: Pinot Grigio, Sauvignon Blanc

Mahón
Type: Semi-hard, cow's milk
Country of Origin: Spain (Balearic Islands)
Wine: Cava, Manzanilla Sherry

Majorero
Type: Semi-hard, goat's milk
Country of Origin: Spain (Canary Islands)
Wine: Cava, Rioja (red)

Malvarosa
Type: Semi-firm, sheep's milk
Country of Origin: Spain (Valencia)
Wine: Monastrell, Tempranillo

Manchego
Type: Soft, sheep's milk

Country of Origin: Spain (La Mancha)
Wine: Cava, Rioja (red)

Manouri
Type: Semi-soft, goat's or sheep's milk
Country of Origin: Greece (Thessalia)
Wine: Agiorgitiko, Moschofilero

Marco Polo
Type: Hard, cow's milk
Country of Origin: United States (Washington)
Wine: Bordeaux (red), Cabernet Sauvignon

Maroilles
Type: Soft, cow's milk
Country of Origin: France (Nord-Pas-de-Calais)
Wine: Bonnezeaux, Gewürztraminer (off-dry)

Mascarpone
Type: Soft-fresh, cow's milk
Country of Origin: Italy (Lombardy)
Wine: Sauvignon Blanc, Sparkling Wine (white)

Melinda Mae
Type: Soft, cow's milk
Country of Origin: United States (Connecticut)

Wine: Beaujolais, Chardonnay (oaked)

Merlot Bellavitano
Type: Semi-hard, cow's milk
Country of Origin: United States (Wisconsin)
Wine: Merlot, Pinot Noir

Mesost
Type: Semi-soft, cow's and goat's milk
Country of Origin: Sweden (Sundbyberg)
Wine: Moscato d'Asti, Riesling Spätlese

Middlebury Blue
Type: Semi-soft, cow's milk
Country of Origin: United States (Vermont)
Wine: Malmsey Madeira, Maury

Milleens
Type: Semi-soft, cow's milk
Country of Origin: Ireland (County Cork)
Wine: Gewürztraminer, Moscato

Mimolette
Type: Semi-hard, cow's milk
Country of Origin: France (Lille)
Wine: Cabernet Sauvignon, Carignan

Minuet

Type: Soft, cow's and goat's milk
Country of Origin: United States (California)
Wine: Prosecco, Provence (rosé)

Mitibleu

Type: Soft, sheep's milk
Country of Origin: Spain (Castilla La Mancha)
Wine: Oloroso Sherry, Riesling

Moliterno al Tartufo

Type: Firm, sheep's milk
Country of Origin: Italy (Sardinia)
Wine: Chianti, Grenache

Montasio

Type: Semi-soft, cow's milk
Country of Origin: Italy (Friuli Venezia Giulia and Veneto)
Wine: Greco di Tufo, Sauvignon Blanc

Monte Enebro

Type: Semi-soft, goat's milk
Country of Origin: Spain (Avila)
Wine: Manzanilla Sherry, Rioja (white)

Monte Festivo
Type: Firm, goat's milk
Country of Origin: United States (Texas)
Wine: Bordeaux (white), Garnacha (rosé)

Monterey Jack
Type: Semi-hard, cow's milk
Country of Origin: United States (California)
Wine: Pinot Noir, Riesling

Montsec
Type: Soft, goat's milk
Country of Origin: Spain (Catalonia)
Wine: Riesling, Sauvignon Blanc

Moosbacher
Type: Semi-hard, cow's milk
Country of Origin: Austria (Styria)
Wine: Anjou (white), Cabernet Sauvignon

Morbier
Type: Soft, cow's milk
Country of Origin: France (Morbier)
Wine: Gewürztraminer, Savagnin

Morlacco del Grappa
Type: Semi-firm, cow's milk
Country of Origin: Italy (Veneto)
Wine: Bardolino, Prosecco

Moses Sleeper
Type: Semi-soft, cow's milk
Country of Origin: United States (Vermont)
Wine: Chardonnay (unoaked), Pinot Noir

Mozzarella Fresca
Type: Soft, cow's or water buffalo's milk
Country of Origin: Italy (Milan)
Wine: Greco di Tufo, Roero Arneis

Mt. Tam
Type: Soft, cow's milk
Country of Origin: United States (California)
Wine: Sauvignon Blanc, Sparkling Wine (white)

Muffato
Type: Semi-hard (blue), cow's milk
Country of Origin: Italy (Veneto)
Wine: Monbazillac, Roero Arneis

Münster
Type: Soft, cow's milk
Country of Origin: France (Bas-Rhin)
Wine: Gewürztraminer, Sparkling Wine (rosé)

Murazzano
Type: Fresh-soft, cow's and goat's milk
Country of Origin: Italy (Murazzano)
Wine: Chardonnay, Verdicchio

Mycella
Type: Soft (blue), cow's milk
Country of Origin: Denmark (Bornholm)
Wine: Chateauneuf-du-Pape (white), Prosecco

Myzithra
Type: Fresh-soft, cow's, goat's and sheep's milk
Country of Origin: Greece (Cyprus)
Wine: Assyrtiko, Crémant d'Alsace

N

Neufchâtel
Type: Soft, cow's milk
Country of Origin: France (Neufchâtel-en-Bray)
Wine: Gewürztraminer, Sancerre

Nevat
Type: Semi-soft, goat's milk
Country of Origin: Spain (Cataluna)
Wine: Pinot Grigio, Sauvignon Blanc

New Moon
Type: Semi-hard, cow's milk
Country of Origin: United States (Washington)
Wine: Pinot Noir, Sparkling Wine (white)

New Woman
Type: Firm, cow's milk
Country of Origin: United States (New York)
Wine: Shiraz, Zinfandel

Nicasio Reserve
Type: Hard, cow's milk

Country of Origin: United States (California)
Wine: Chardonnay, Roussanne

Nickjack
Type: Semi-soft, cow's milk
Country of Origin: United States (Tennessee)
Wine: Côtes-du-Rhône (red), Shiraz

Niolo
Type: Soft, sheep's milk
Country of Origin: France (Albertacce)
Wine: Chardonnay, Provence (rosé)

Nocetto di Capra
Type: Semi-soft, goat's milk
Country of Origin: Italy (Lombardy)
Wine: Pinot Grigio, Roero Arneis

Nokkelost
Type: Semi-hard, cow's milk
Country of Origin: Scandinavia (Norway)
Wine: Amarone della Valpolicella, Valpolicella Ripasso

North Sea
Type: Hard, cow's milk
Country of Origin: Demark (North Jutland)

Wine: Bordeaux (red), Cabernet Sauvignon

Nuvola di Pecora
Type: Firm, sheep's milk
Country of Origin: Italy (Emilia-Romana)
Wine: Cabernet Sauvignon, Nero d'Avola

O

Oaxaca
Type: Semi-hard, cow's milk
Country of Origin: Mexico (Oaxaca)
Wine: Chenin Blanc, Dolcetto

Ocooch Mountain
Type: Semi-hard, sheep's milk
Country of Origin: United States (Wisconsin)
Wine: Grenache (red), Pinot Blanc

O'Kéfir
Type: Firm, cow's milk
Country of Origin: Canada (Chaudière-Appalaches)
Wine: Grüner Veltliner, Roero Arneis

Old Amsterdam
Type: Firm, cow's milk
Country of Origin: Netherlands (Amsterdan)
Wine: Bordeaux, Cabernet Sauvignon

Original Blue
Type: Semi-soft, cow's milk

Country of Origin: United States (California)
Wine: Icewine, Moscato d'Asti

Oregon Blue

Type: Semi-soft, cow's milk
Country of Origin: United States (Oregon)
Wine: Pinot Noir, Riesling

Oregonzola

Type: Soft, cow's milk
Country of Origin: United States (Oregon)
Wine: Pinot Noir, Shiraz

Oscypek

Type: Semi-hard, cow's and sheep's milk
Country of Origin: Poland (Tatra Mountains)
Wine: Riesling, Sparkling Wine (white)

Ossau-Iraty

Type: Semi-hard, sheep's milk
Country of Origin: France (Béarn and Iraty)
Wine: Amontillado Sherry, Merlot

P

Pag Island
Type: Hard, sheep's milk
Country of Origin: Croatia (Island of Pag)
Wine: Cabernet Sauvignon, Pelješac (red)

Panela
Type: Fresh-firm, cow's milk
Country of Origin: Mexico (Tapalpa)
Wine: Chardonnay, Shiraz (rosé)

Panquehue
Type: Semi-soft, cow's milk
Country of Origin: Chile (Aconcagua)
Wine: Chardonnay, Sauvignon Blanc

Parmigiano Reggiano
Type: Hard, cow's milk
Country of Origin: Italy (Bologna)
Wine: Barolo, Cabernet Sauvignon

Parrano
Type: Hard, cow's milk

Country of Origin: Netherlands (Het Groene Hart)
Wine: Pinot Noir, Tawny Port

PataCabra

Type: Soft, goat's milk
Country of Origin: Spain (Aragon)
Wine: Cava, Riesling

Pavé d'Affinois

Type: Soft, cow's milk
Country of Origin: France (Loire)
Wine: Chardonnay, Sparkling Wine (white)

Pecorino

Type: Hard, sheep's milk
Country of Origin: Italy (Lazio, Sardinia, and Tuscany)
Wine: Cabernet Sauvignon, Chianti

Pecorino Foglie di Noce

Type: Hard, sheep's milk
Country of Origin: Italy (Emilia-Romagna)
Wine: Pecorino, Sagrantino di Montefalco

Pecorino Pepato

Type: Semi-firm, sheep's milk
Country of Origin: Italy (Sicily)

Wine: Montepulciano d'Abruzzo, Velletri (red)

Pecorino Romano
Type: Hard, sheep's milk
Country of Origin: Italy (Lazio, Sardinia, and Tuscany)
Wine: Amarone della Valpolicella, Merlot

Pecorino Siciliano
Type: Firm, sheep's milk
Country of Origin: Italy (Sicily)
Wine: Cabernet Sauvignon, Taurasi Riserva

Pecorino Toscano
Type: Semi-firm, sheep's milk
Country of Origin: Italy (Tuscany)
Wine: Barbera, Cabernet Sauvignon

Pélardon des Cévennes
Type: Soft, goat's milk
Country of Origin: France (Languedoc)
Wine: Chablis, Saint-Émilion (red)

Perlagrigia Sottocenere al Tartufo
Type: Soft, cow's milk
Country of Origin: Italy (Veneto)
Wine: Barbera d'Alba, Pinot Noir

Petit Cendré

Type: Firm, goat's milk

Country of Origin: Canada (Laval)

Wine: Grenache Blanc, Sauvignon Blanc

Piave

Type: Hard, cow's milk

Country of Origin: Italy (Veneto)

Wine: Chardonnay, Merlot

Picodon

Type: Soft, goat's milk

Country of Origin: France (Ardèche and Drome)

Wine: Bourdeaux (white), Côtes-du-Rhône (Rosé)

Pleasant Ridge Reserve

Type: Semi-hard, cow's milk

Country of Origin: United States (Wisconsin)

Wine: Cabernet Sauvignon, Moscato d'Asti

Poco Rojo

Type: Soft, sheep's milk

Country of Origin: United States (Idaho)

Wine: Sauvignon Blanc, Sparkling Wine (white)

Pont-l'Évêque
Type: Soft, cow's milk
Country of Origin: France (Pont-l'Évêque)
Wine: Bourdeaux (red), Burgundy (red)

Porter Cheddar
Type: Semi-hard, cow's milk
Country of Origin: Ireland (Limerick)
Wine: Irish Porter Beer, Shiraz, Zinfandel

Port Salut
Type: Semi-hard, cow's milk
Country of Origin: France (Pays de la Loire)
Wine: Grüner Veltliner, Pinot Noir

Pouligny Saint-Pierre
Type: Soft, cow's milk
Country of Origin: France (Indre)
Wine: Pouilly Fumé, Sparkling Wine (white)

Préféré des Nos Montagnes
Type: Soft, cow's milk
Country of Origin: France (Jura)
Wine: Crémant du Jura, Gamay

Prima Donna
Type: Hard, cow's milk
Country of Origin: Netherlands (Holland)
Wine: Chianti, Pinot Noir

Promontory
Type: Semi-firm, cow's milk
Country of Origin: United States (Utah)
Wine: Cabernet Sauvignon, Nero d'Avola

Providence
Type: Semi-soft, goat's milk
Country of Origin: United States (North Carolina)
Wine: Chablis, Pinot Noir

Provoleta
Type: Semi-hard, water buffalo's milk
Country of Origin: Argentina (Costanera Norte)
Wine: Malbec, Sparkling Wine (rosé)

Provolone
Type: Semi-hard, cow's milk
Country of Origin: Italy (Po Valley Region)
Wine: Greco di Tufo, Syrah

Provolone Valpadana
Type: Semi-hard, cow's milk
Country of Origin: Italy (Milan to Udine)
Wine: Cabernet Sauvignon, Merlot

Prufrock
Type: Semi-soft, cow's milk
Country of Origin: United States (Massachusetts)
Wine: Cabernet Sauvignon, Port (white)

P'tit Basque
Type: Hard, sheep's milk
Country of Origin: France (Pyrenees)
Wine: Côtes-du-Rhône (red), Pinot Noir

Purple Haze
Type: Soft-fresh, goat's milk
Country of Origin: United States (California)
Wine: Provence (rosé), Riesling

Purple Moon Cheddar
Type: Semi-hard, cow's milk
Country of Origin: United States (California)
Wine: Cabernet Sauvignon, Sparkling Wine (rosé)

Q

Quadrello di Bufala
Type: Semi-soft, water buffalo's milk
Country of Origin: Italy (Lombardy)
Wine: Riesling, Vermentino

Quartirolo Lombardo
Type: Soft, cow's milk
Country of Origin: Italy (Lombardy)
Wine: Bardolino, Colli di Luni Rosso

Queso Azul
Type: Semi-soft (blue), goat's milk
Country of Origin: Spain (Andalucía)
Wine: Cava, Priorat (red)

Queso Blanco
Type: Fresh-soft, cow's and goat's milk
Country of Origin: Mexico (Guanajuato)
Wine: Cava, Chardonnay

Queso Bola de Ocosingo
Type: Fresh, cow's milk

Country of Origin: Mexico (Chiapas)
Wine: Cava, Pinot Grigio

Queso de La Serena
Type: Soft, sheep's milk
Country of Origin: Spain (Extremadura)
Wine: Albariño, Cava

Queso de Nata de Cantabria
Type: Semi-soft, cow's milk
Country of Origin: Spain (Cantrabia)
Wine: Cava, Manzanilla Sherry

Queso de Poro de Balancán
Type: Fresh, cow's milk
Country of Origin: Mexico (Balancán)
Wine: Chardonnay, Sparkling Wine (white)

R

Raclette
Type: Soft, cow's milk
Country of Origin: France and Switzerland (Valais)
Wine: Pinot Gris, Sauvignon Blanc

Ragged Point
Type: Soft, cow's milk
Country of Origin: United States (California)
Wine: Pinot Noir, Prosecco

Raspberry Ale Bellavitano
Type: Hard, cow's milk
Country of Origin: United States (Wiconsin)
Wine: Merlot, Riesling

Rasquera
Type: Semi-soft, cow's milk
Country of Origin: Italy (Piemond)
Wine: Barbera d'Alba, Chianti

Rassembleu
Type: Firm (blue), cow's milk

Country of Origin: Canada (Laurentians)
Wine: Chenin Blanc (off-dry), Riesling (off-dry)

Reading
Type: Semi-soft, cow's milk
Country of Origin: United States (Vermont)
Wine: Bordeaux (white), Chenin Blanc

Reblochon
Type: Semi-hard, cow's milk
Country of Origin: France (Haute-Savoie)
Wine: Burgundy (white), Pinot Noir

Red Dragon
Type: Semi-soft, cow's milk
Country of Origin: United Kingdom (Abergavenny)
Wine: Pinot Noir, Shiraz

Red Hawk
Type: Soft, cow's milk
Country of Origin: United States (California)
Wine: Gewürztraminer, Sparkling Wine (white)

Red Witch
Type: Firm, cow's milk
Country of Origin: Switzerland (St. Gallen)

Wine: Gewürztraminer, Pinot Gris

Reggianito
Type: Hard, cow's milk
Country of Origin: Argentina (Provincia de Córdoba)
Wine: Sauvignon Blanc, Sparkling Wine (white)

Requesón
Type: Fresh, goat's milk
Country of Origin: Spain (Alicante)
Wine: Cava, Chardonnay

Reypenaer
Type: Firm, cow's milk
Country of Origin: Netherlands (Utrecht)
Wine: Burgundy (red), Merlot

Ricotta Salata
Type: Soft-fresh, sheep's milk
Country of Origin: Italy (Sicily)
Wine: Lambrusco (white), Pinot Grigio

Ridder
Type: Semi-hard, cow's milk
Country of Origin: Scandinavia (Norway)
Wine: Pinot noir, Riesling

Roaring Forties Blue
Type: Semi-soft, cow's milk
Country of Origin: Australia (Tasmania)
Wine: Sauternes, Shiraz

Robiola Bosina
Type: Soft, cow's and sheep's milk
Country of Origin: Italy (Piedmont)
Wine: Dolcetto, Prosecco

Robiola Piedmont
Type: Soft-ripened, goat's milk
Country of Origin: Italy (Piedmont)
Wine: Chardonnay, Soave

Robiola di Roccaverano
Type: Soft-fresh, goat's milk
Country of Origin: Italy (Piedmont)
Wine: Chardonnay, Roero Arneis

Rocamadour
Type: Soft, goat's milk
Country of Origin: France (Perigord)
Wine: Burgundy (red), Jurançon (white)

Rockets Robiola
Type: Soft, cow's milk
Country of Origin: United States (North Carolina)
Wine: Barbera, Nebbiolo

Rogue River Blue
Type: Soft, cow's milk
Country of Origin: United States (Oregon)
Wine: Cabernet Franc, Sauternes

Romao
Type: Firm, sheep's milk
Country of Origin: Spain (Castilla La Mancha)
Wine: Albillo, Cava

Roncal
Type: Hard, sheep's milk
Country of Origin: Spain (Navarra)
Wine: Cava, Navarra (red)

Roomano Pradera
Type: Hard, cow's milk
Country of Origin: Netherlands (Holland)
Wine: Gamay, Pinot Noir

Roomkaas

Type: Semi-soft, cow's milk
Country of Origin: Netherlands (Holland)
Wine: Chenin Blanc, Riesling

Roquefort

Type: Soft, sheep's milk
Country of Origin: France (Roquefort-sur-Soulzon)
Wine: Cabernet Sauvignon, Sauternes

Roves de Garrigues

Type: Soft, goat's milk
Country of Origin: France (Midi Pyrénées)
Wine: Pinot Gris, Provence (rosé)

S

Sage and Herb Cheddar
Type: Hard, cow's milk
Country of Origin: United States (Vermont)
Wine: Provence (rosé), Sparkling Wine (rosé)

Sage Derby
Type: Semi-hard, cow's milk
Country of Origin: England (Derbyshire)
Wine: Sauvignon Blanc, Vinho Verde (white)

Saint Agur
Type: Soft (blue), cow's milk
Country of Origin: France (Auvergne)
Wine: Chardonnay, Tawny Port

Saint Albray
Type: Soft, cow's milk
Country of Origin: France (Aquitaine)
Wine: Chianti, Pinot Noir

Saint André
Type: Semi-soft, cow's milk

Country of Origin: France (Normandy)
Wine: Syrah (rosé), Sauternes

Saint Angel
Type: Soft, cow's milk
Country of Origin: France (Rhone-Alps)
Wine: Champagne, Saint-Émillion (red)

Sainte Maure de Touraine
Type: Soft, goat's milk
Country of Origin: France (Touraine)
Wine: Cava, Chenin Blanc

Saint Félicien
Type: Soft, cow's milk
Country of Origin: France (Rhône-Aps)
Wine: Chinon (red), Côtes-du-Rhône (red)

Saint George
Type: Firm, cow's milk
Country of Origin: United States (California)
Wine: Amontillado Sherry, Riesling

Saint-Marcellin
Type: Soft, cow's milk
Country of Origin: France (Isère)

Wine: Grüner Veltliner, Sémillon

Saint Nectaire
Type: Semi-soft, cow's milk
Country of Origin: France (Auvergne)
Wine: Beaujolais, Côtes d'Auvergne (red)

Saint Paulin
Type: Semi-hard, cow's milk
Country of Origin: France (Saint Paulin)
Wine: Beaujolais (red), Riesling

Salers
Type: Semi-hard, cow's milk
Country of Origin: France (Salers)
Wine: Bourdeaux (white), Pinot Noir

San Andreas
Type: Hard, sheep's milk
Country of Origin: United States (California)
Wine: Chianti, Pinot Noir

San Geronimo
Type: Semi-soft, cow's milk
Country of Origin: United States (California)
Wine: Chardonnay, Saint-Joseph (white)

San Simon
Type: Semi-soft, cow's milk
Country of Origin: Spain (Galicia)
Wine: Cava, Mencía

São Jorge
Type: Semi-hard, cow's milk
Country of Origin: Portugal (Azores)
Wine: Pinot Grigio, Pinot Noir

Sapore Mitica
Type: Hard, cow's milk
Country of Origin: Italy (Veneto)
Wine: Amarone della Valpolicella, Franciacorta

Sardo Argentino
Type: Semi-hard, cow's milk
Country of Origin: Argentina (Folgoso Bardullas)
Wine: Viognier, Torrontés

Savage
Type: Semi-soft, cow's milk
Country of Origin: United States (Vermont)
Wine: Gewürztraminer, Riesling

Sawtooth
Type: Semi-soft, cow's milk
Country of Origin: United States (Washington)
Wine: Sparkling Wine (rosé), Touraine (red)

Sbrinz
Type: Hard, cow's milk
Country of Origin: Switzerland (Lucerne)
Wine: Chardonnay (oaked), Grüner Veltliner

Scamorza
Type: Semi-hard, cow's and sheep's milk
Country of Origin: Italy (Apulia)
Wine: Orvieto, Pinot Grigio

Schallenberg
Type: Firm, cow's milk
Country of Origin: Switzerland (Schallenberg)
Wine: Riesling, Sangiovese

Schnebelhorn
Type: Hard, cow's milk
Country of Origin: Switzerland (St. Gallen Province)
Wine: Gewürztraminer, Pinot Gris

Seascape
Type: Semi-hard, cow's and goat's milk
Country of Origin: United States (California)
Wine: Cabernet Sauvignon, Zinfandel

Selles sur Cher
Type: Soft, goat's milk
Country of Origin: France (Sologne)
Wine: Provence (rosé), Sauvignon Blanc

Serpa
Type: Semi-soft, sheep's milk
Country of Origin: Portugal (Alentejo)
Wine: 10 Years Old Tawny Port, Riesling

Serra da Estrela
Type: Semi-hard, sheep's milk
Country of Origin: Portugal (Serra da Estrela)
Wine: Dão (white), Tawny Port

Shepherd's Hope
Type: Soft-fresh, sheep's milk
Country of Origin: United States (Minnesota)
Wine: Beaujoulais, Sémillon

Shropshire Blue
Type: Semi-soft, cow's milk
Country of Origin: Great Britain (Nottinghamshire)
Wine: Pinot Noir, Tawny Port

Sleeping Beauty
Type: Semi-hard, cow's milk
Country of Origin: United States (Washington)
Wine: Merlot, Nebbiolo

Smoked Cheddar
Type: Semi-hard, cow's milk
Country of Origin: United States (Vermont)
Wine: Garnacha, Shiraz

Sottocenere al Tartufo
Type: Semi-hard, cow's milk
Country of Origin: Italy (Veneto)
Wine: Barbera, Sparkling Wine (white)

Squacquerone
Type: Fresh, cow's milk
Country of Origin: Italy (Bologna)
Wine: Chardonnay, Franciacorta

Stichelton

Type: Semi-soft, cow's milk
Country of Origin: United Kingdom (Nottinghamshire)
Wine: Riesling, Sparkling Wine (white)

Stilton Blue

Type: Soft, cow's milk
Country of Origin: United Kingdom (Cambridgeshire)
Wine: Tawny Port, Tokaji

Stilton White

Type: Soft, cow's milk
Country of Origin: United Kingdom (Cambridgeshire)
Wine: Chenin Blanc, Sauvignon Blanc

Stracciatella

Type: Soft-fresh, cow's milk
Country of Origin: Italy (Foggia)
Wine: Pinot Grigio, Viognier

Swiss

Type: Hard, cow's milk
Country of Origin: United States (Ohio)
Wine: Pinot Noir, Vidal Blanc

T

Taleggio
Type: Soft, cow's milk
Country of Origin: Italy (Bergamo)
Wine: Franciacorta, Soave

Taliah
Type: Firm, sheep's milk
Country of Origin: Canada (Centre-du-Québec)
Wine: Carménère, Gamay

Taramundi
Type: Semi-hard, cow's, goat's Milk
Country of Origin: Spain (Taramundi)
Wine: Ribeiro (white), Sauvignon Blanc

Tarentaise
Type: Hard, cow's milk
Country of Origin: United States (Vermont)
Wine: Cabernet Sauvignon, Pinot Noir

Teleme
Type: Semi-soft, cow's milk

Country of Origin: United States (California)
Wine: Pinot Blanc, Viognier

Tennessee Whiskey Bellavitano

Type: Firm, cow's milk
Country of Origin: United States (Wisconsin)
Wine: Chardonnay, Sauvignon Blanc

Tête de Moine

Type: Semi-hard, cow's milk
Country of Origin: Switzerland (Berna)
Wine: Pinot Grigio, Pinot Noir

The Blue Jay

Type: Semi-hard (blue), cow's milk
Country of Origin: United States (Wisconsin)
Wine: Riesling (off-dry), Vinho Verde (white)

The Moon Rabbit

Type: Semi-hard, cow's milk
Country of Origin: United States (Wisconsin)
Wine: Gewürztraminer, Sparkling Wine (white)

The Rattlesnake Cheddar

Type: Semi-hard, cow's milk
Country of Origin: United States (Wisconsin)

Wine: Moscato d'Asti, Viognier

Thomasville Tomme
Type: Semi–hard, cow's milk
Country of Origin: United States (Georgia)
Wine: Pinot Noir, Shiraz

Three Milk Gouda
Type: Semi–soft, cow's, goat's and sheep's milk
Country of Origin: United States (New York)
Wine: Chenin Blanc, Riesling

Ticklemore
Type: Semi–hard, goat's milk
Country of Origin: England (Sharpham)
Wine: Provence (rosé), Pinot Gris

Tintern
Type: Soft, cow's milk
Country of Origin: Wales (Monmouthshire)
Wine: Muscadet, Pinot Noir

Toma Piedmontese
Type: Semi–soft, cow's milk
Country of Origin: Italy (Piedmont)
Wine: Soave, Verdicchio

Tomme de Savoie

Type: Semi-soft, cow's milk

Country of Origin: France (Savoie)

Wine: Pinot Gris, Riesling

Tomme Vaudoise

Type: Soft, Cow's milk

Country of Origin: Switzerland (Vaud and Geneva)

Wine: Chasselas, Gamay

Torta del Casar

Type: Semi-hard, sheep's milk

Country of Origin: Spain (Extremadura)

Wine: Cava, Oloroso Sherry

Touvelle Original

Type: Semi-hard, cow's milk

Country of Origin: United States (Oregon)

Wine: Chardonnay (oaked), Sparkling Wine (white)

Trillium

Type: Soft, cow's milk

Country of Origin: United States (Indiana)

Wine: Chardonnay, Pinot Noir

Tronchón
Type: Semi-soft, cow's, goat's and sheep's milk
Country of Origin: Spain (Murcia)
Wine: Cava, Chardonnay (oaked)

Truffle Tremor
Type: Soft, goat's cheese
Country of Origin: United States (California)
Wine: Sancerre, Verdejo

Tumalo Tomme
Type: Firm, goat's milk
Country of Origin: United States (Oregon)
Wine: Merlot, Pinot Noir

U

Ubriaco all'Amarone
Type: Semi-hard, cow's milk
Country of Origin: Italy (Veneto)
Wine: Amarone della Valpolicella, Valpolicella Ripasso

Ubriaco al Prosecco
Type: Semi-hard, cow's milk
Country of Origin: Italy (Veneto)
Wine: Chianti, Prosecco

Ubriaco di Raboso
Type: Semi-hard, cow's milk
Country of Origin: Italy (Veneto)
Wine: Cabernet Sauvignon, Raboso Piave

Ubriaco Rosso
Type: Semi-hard, cow's milk
Country of Origin: Italy (Veneto)
Wine: Cabernet sauvignon, Merlot

Ulloa
Type: Semi-soft, cow's milk

Country of Origin: Spain (Galicia)
Wine: Albariño, Vinho Verde (white)

Up in Smoke
Type: Soft-fresh, goat's milk
Country of Origin: United States (Oregon)
Wine: Chenin Blanc, Riesling

Urgèlia
Type: Semi-firm, cow's milk
Country of Origin: Spain (Catalonia)
Wine: Cava, Garnacha

V

Valbert
Type: Firm, cow's milk
Country of Origin: Canada (Saguenay-Lac-Saint-Jean)
Wine: Fumé Blanc, Riesling

Vacherin Mont d'Or
Type: Soft, cow's milk
Country of Origin: Switzerland (Les Charbonnières)
Wine: Gewürztraminer, Riesling

Valdeón
Type: Semi-soft, cow's and goat's milk
Country of Origin: Spain (Castilla Leon)
Wine: Grüner Veltliner, Sauternes

Valençay
Type: Soft, goat's milk
Country of Origin: France (Loire)
Wine: Chenin Blanc, Loire (white)

Valençay Frais
Type: Soft-fresh, goat's milk

Country of Origin: France (Loire)
Wine: Chardonnay, Sparkling Wine (white)

Valentine
Type: Soft-fresh, sheep's milk
Country of Origin: United States (Oregon)
Wine: Chenin Blanc, Riesling

Vampire Slayer
Type: Firm, cow's milk
Country of Origin: United States (Oregon)
Wine: Gewürztraminer, Riesling

Vermont Shepherd
Type: Firm, sheep's milk
Country of Origin: United States (Vermont)
Wine: Chardonnay, Oloroso Sherry

Vigneron
Type: Soft, goat's milk
Country of Origin: Australia (South Australia)
Wine: Chardonnay, Sauvignon Blanc

Vlimeux
Type: Semi-firm, cow's and sheep's milk
Country of Origin: Canada (Bas-Saint-Laurent)

Wine: Grenache (red), Mencia

W

Wensleydale
Type: Hard, cow's and sheep's milk
Country of Origin: United Kingdom (North Yorkshire)
Wine: Burgundy (red), Tawny Port

White Diamond
Type: Soft, goat's cheese
Country of Origin: United States (Vermont)
Wine: Chenin Blanc, Fumé Blanc

Wilde Weide
Type: Hard, cow's milk
Country of Origin: Netherlands (Zwanburgerpolder)
Wine: Riesling, Shiraz

Willoughby
Type: Semi-soft, cow's milk
Country of Origin: United States (Vermont)
Wine: Chinon, Vouvray

Wischago
Type: Hard, sheep's milk

Country of Origin: United States (Wisconsin)
Wine: Bordeaux (white), Madiran (red)

Wrångebäck
Type: Hard, cow's milk
Country of Origin: Sweden (Västra Götaland)
Wine: Jura (white), Sparkling Wine (white)

Wyfe of Bath
Type: Semi-hard, cow's milk
Country of Origin: England (Bath)
Wine: Manzanilla Sherry, Tawny Port 10 Years Old

Y

Yale Creek
Type: Hard, cow's milk
Country of Origin: United States (Oregon)
Wine: Amontillado Sherry, Merlot

Yorkshire Blue
Type: Soft, cow's milk
Country of Origin: England (North Yorkshire)
Wine: Late Harvest Madeleine Angevine, Tokaji

Z

Zacharie Cloutier
Type: Firm, sheep's milk
Country of Origin: Canada (Eastern Townships)
Wine: Bobal, Carignan

Zamorano
Type: Hard, sheep's milk
Country of Origin: Spain (Castilla Y León)
Wine: Garnacha, Tempranillo

Zelu Koloria
Type: Firm, sheep's milk
Country of Origin: France (Aquitaine)
Wine: Jurançon Moelleux, Tawny Port

Ziege Zacke Blue
Type: Soft, cow's and goat's milk
Country of Origin: United States (Wisconsin)
Wine: Pinot Noir, Syrah

Zimbro
Type: Soft, sheep's milk

Country of Origin: Portugal (Serra da Estrela)
Wine: Rioja Crianza, 10 Years Old Tawny Port

TIPS FOR CHEESE BOARDS AND SPREADS

A cheese board or a spread (several boards or plates) doesn't have to be too elaborate but it should be attractive and inviting.

Cheese served in a wooden tray, platter or pizza paddle is more appealing but you can also use ceramic platers (unrimmed) in different colors and shapes, a pedestal cake stand or a marble board as long as it will be easy to cut the cheese on it.

Don't overcrowd the board, your guests will need space to cut the cheese.

Take the cheese out of the fridge 30 minutes before the time you will serve them. The low temperature affects the cheese texture, aromas and taste. Take the cheese out of the package but leave the rim – remove it only if it is wax.

Don't serve a pungent and a soft cheese side by side to avoid mixing the flavors.

You can cut the cheese – mainly hard cheeses that are difficult to cut – in small wedges, cubes, squares, rectangular, or triangles, make sure the sizes are approximately the same, about ¼ inches. You can also crumbled the hard cheese. Cut them right before the time you intent to serve so they will not dry out. Have cheese forks or wood picks available to pick up the cheese or the fruit slices.

Serve fresh cheeses whole.

Cheese labels are a nice way to identify them – I like little flags with the cheese name and country.

Have water with and without gas available. You can place the bottles in an ice bucket – don't forget to set water glasses nearby.

Leftover cheese should be wrapped separately and put in the refrigerator.

HOW TO ASSEMBLE A BOARD

When planning a board or a spread, first you should choose a theme: the wheater, the mood, a country, a state, by the fire, by the pool, romantic or whatever feels right for that day or night. Will the cheese be the center of attention or the wine will reign? Based on your theme choose the cheese and the wine from the pairing suggestions. Add your accompaniments. Make a list and buy everything you need to set a beautiful and inviting board! The possibilities are endless.

To assemble a board start by placing the cheese leaving the center of the board empty. Put the charcuterie around it and fill in the blank spaces and the center with fruit, nuts and last the bread and crackers. Finish with some garnishes...

Accompaniments

Bread and Crackers

- Baguette, rustic loaf, Italian, sourdough, rye... or other plain bread that you like.

- Plain crackers, Triscuits, grissinis, pita crackers,

mini toasts, bruschetta toasts, plain bagel chips...

Charcuterie
- Go for all your favorites – sausage (sliced), Prosciutto di Parma, copaccola, copa, sopressata, culatello, bresaola...

Nuts and Dried Fruit
- Almonds (toasted), Brazilian nuts, pecan halves, walnuts, raw cashews, dried apricots, dried plums, dried persimmons, dried cherries, dried apples....

Fresh Fruit
- Red and white seedless grapes, apple, pear, pomegranate (wedges), figs (halved), kiwi (halved). Apple and pear slices should be dipped in water with a little bit of honey to avoid oxidation.

Pickles
- Cornichons, black and green olives. Olives with pits have a better flavor - place an empty bowl nearby for pits.

Spreads
- Fig and apricot jam, honey and honeycomb, pâté, tapenade, chutney, mustard...

Garnishes

– You can decorate the spread or cheese board with grape leaves, fig leaves, lemon and orange slices, kumquads. You can use also edible flowers, seasonal greens, fresh herbs like dill, thyme and rosemary... Try to add different colors and use your creativity!

AMOUNTS TO BUY

Cheese:

- For a Happy Hour – 1.5 oz of each cheese per person.

- For dessert – 1 oz of each cheese per person.

- If the cheese is the main attraction – 7 oz of cheese per person.

Charcuterie:

- For a Happy Hour – 1.5 oz of each meat per person.

- For a meal – 7 oz of meat per person.

Wine:

To be on the safe side – half a bottle for each guest. But always have some extra bottles in case you will need them. Some guests drink more than others and that way you will not run out of wine.

WINE SERVICE

Try to serve the wine close to its correct temperature. The temperature inside the refrigerator is at or below 40°F and the freezer temperature at or below 0°F.

Sparkling wine: 41-45° F. It should be served ice cold. The best way to get to the right temperature is to place in an ice bucket for 30 minutes or up to 2 hours in the fridge.

Light Bodied Whites (Chenin Blanc, Pinot Grigio, Sauvignon Blanc, Riesling...): 45-49° F. It should be served cold. 1 ½ hours in the fridge.

Full-Bodied Whites and Rosés (Albariño, Chardonnay, Trebbiano, Viognier...): 50-55° F. 1 hour in the fridge.

Light and medium bodied Reds (Beaujolais, Chianti, Dolcetto, Pinot Noir...): 54-60° F. It should be served cool. ¾ to 1 hour in the fridge.

Full-Bodied Reds (Cabernet Sauvignon, Malbec, Merlot, Tempranillo...): 60-65° F. 25 minutes in the fridge.

Dessert wine: 43-46° F. 2 hours in the fridge.

Fortified wines (Port, Sherry, Madeira, Marsala...): 56-68° F. 30 minutes in the fridge.

TASTY IDEIAS....

Blue Cheese Board

Make sure your guests like blue cheese - not everybody likes them.

Cheeses:
1.5 oz of each cheese per person
Danablu
Gorgonzola
Roquefort

Wine Suggestions:
Prosecco pairs well with all the cheeses
Amarone or Banyuls pairs well with Gorgonzola and Danablu
Cabernet Sauvignon or Sauternes pairs well with Roquefort

Accompaniments:
Prosciutto di Parma, grissinis, thin baguette slices, plain crackers in different form and textures. Decorate the board with apple and pear slices, honey or honeycomb, fig jam and toasted walnuts.

Cheese and Charcuterie Board

Cheeses:
1.5 oz of each cheese per person
Brie
Chèvre
Ponte L'Évêque

Meats:
Bresaola, Capicola, Copa, Culatello, Sopressata...
Prosciutto di Parma
Sausage Slices

Wine Suggestions:
Sparkling wine (white) pairs well with all cheeses and meats

Pinot Noir pairs well with Brie, Ponte L'Évêque, Bresaola, Capicola, Copa, Culatello and Sopressata

Barbera pairs well with Prosciutto di Parma
Riesling pairs well with Sausage

Accompaniments:
Thin baguette slices, grissinis, bruschetta toasts, Triscuit crakers in diferente flavors and plain crackers. Decorate with bunches of seedless grapes, apple and pear slices, pomegranates (halved), figs (halved), edible

flowers, dried apricots, black and green olives and walnuts.

Cheese Spread

Cheeses:

1.5 oz of each cheese per person

Boursin

Fontina

Grana Padano

Gruyère

Livarot

Montsec

Oregon Blue

Wine Suggestions:

The amount of wine will depend in how much your guests drink. I suggest one bottle of each.

Prosecco pairs well with all cheeses

Pinot Gris pairs well with Gruyère and Livarot

Pinot Noir pairs well with Boursin and Fontina

Riesling pairs well with Montsec and Oregon Blue

Accompaniments:

Thin baguette slices, mini toasts and crackers in different shapes, sizes and flavors, roast beef or thin slices of filet mignon. Decorate with figs, strawberries, dried apricots, walnuts, raw cashews, black and green olives and sopressata (sliced).

French Board

Cheeses:
1.5 oz of each cheese per person
Brie
Brillat-Savarin
Camembert

Wine Suggestions:
All cheeses pair well with Champagne, Sparkling Wine (white) or Prosecco (rosé)

Accompaniments:
Pâté de Campagne, French baguette slices, pumpernickel bread, water crackers, red seedless grapes, apple and pear slices, figs (halved), dried apricots, walnuts, almonds and blackberry jam. Decorate with small edible flowers in beautiful colors.

Italian Board

Cheeses:
1.5 oz of each cheese per person
Parmigiano Reggiano
Grana Padano
Gorgonzola Dolce
Provolone Valpadana

Wine Suggestions:
All cheeses pair well with Prosecco
Cabernet Sauvignon pairs well with Parmigiano Reggiano and Provolone Valpadana
Gorgonzola Dolce pairs well with Banyuls

Accompaniments:
Grissinis rolled in Prosciutto di Parma (do it right before serving otherwise the grissinis might turn soft), sliced sopressata, baguette thin sliced (or use other bread that you like), plain crackers in different form and textures and black and green olives. Decore the board with red, white seedless grapes and grape leaves.

Oregon Spread

Cheeses:
1.5 oz of each cheese per person
Cow's Milk Cheeses: Buncon in Bloom, Callisto and Hannah (cow's and sheep's milk) and Hapyard Cheddar
Goat's Milk Cheeses: Elk Mountain, Iris and Up in Smoke
Sheep's Milk Cheeses: Valentine
Blue Cheeses: Oregon Blue, Oregonzola

Meats:
1.5 oz per meat per person
Capacollo (sliced)
Smoked Salmon (sliced)
Prosciutto di Parma (rolled up)
Sopressata (sliced)

Wine Suggestions:
Sparkling Wine (rosé) pairs well with all cheeses and meats
Pinot Noir pairs well with Buncom in Bloom, Callisto, Hannah, Oregon Blue and Oregonzola
Shiraz pairs well with Elk Mountain and Oregonzola
Riesling pairs well with Hapyard Cheddar, Iris, Oregon Blue and Valentine

Accompaniments:

Thin baguette slices or other bread of your choice, grissinis, bruschetta toasts, crackers, almonds, walnuts, dried apricots, cornichons, fig jam, honey, honeycomb and olive tapenade. Decorate with figs, grapes, pomegranate, dried oranges and lemons slices.

Summer Board by the Pool

Cheeses:
1.5 oz of each cheese per person
Chèvre
Camembert
Gouda

Meats:
Prosciutto di Parma (rolled)
Sopressata (sliced)

Wine Suggestions:
Sparkling Wine (white) – keep it in an ice bucket

Accompaniments:
Crackers in different shapes and sizes, watermelon triangles, sliced apples, cherries, strawberries, dried apricots, walnuts, pecans and cashews.

Whole Brie Cheese

1.5 oz per person
The Brie size will depend on many guests you will be serving.

Wine Suggestions:
Champagne or Sparkling Wine (white) and/or
Pinot Noir and/or
Sauvignon Blanc

Accompaniments:
Thin baguette slices, plain crackers, apple and pears slices, fig jam and honey or honeycomb. Decorate with dried apricots, red seedless grapes, rosemary springs, pecan halves, Prosciutto di Parma, pomegranate wedges and walnuts.

Winter Board by the Fireplace

Cheeses:
1.5 oz of each cheese per person
Boscheto al Tartufo
Manchego
Parmigiano Reggiano

Wine Suggestions:
Cava pairs well with all cheeses
Barolo pairs well with Boscheto al Tartufo and Parmigiano Reggiano
Rioja (red) pairs well with Manchego

Accompaniments:
Thin baguette slices or other bread of your choice, grissinis wrapped in Prosciutto di Parma (do it right before serving otherwise the grissinis might turn soft), caponata, green or black olives – or both, dried apricots, figs and almonds. If you like something sweet you can add quince jam which goes very well with the Manchego. Decorate with red and white seedless grapes.

New Year's Eve Board

Cheeses:
1.5 oz of each cheese per person
Brie
Pavé d'Affinois

Wine Suggestions:
The evening pairs well with Champagne, Prosecco (rosé) and Sparkling Wine (white or rosé – or both!)

Accompaniments:
Blinis, caviar, sour cream, smoked salmon (thinly sliced), pumpernickel bread and crackers. Decorate with grape leaves and red and white seedless grapes.

Valentine's Day Board

Cheeses:
1.5 oz of each cheese per person
Brie (cut in a heart shape)
Cremont
Délice de Bourgogne

Wine Suggestions:
Champagne, Sparkling Wine (white) and Vinho Verde (white) pair well with all cheeses

Burgundy (red) and Pinot Noir pair well with Brie and Délice de Bourgogne

Accompaniments:
Water crackers and heart shaped crackers, ciabatta slices, smoked salmon wrapped breadsticks, almonds, pecans, cherries, strawberries, raspberries and apple slices. Decorate with wrapped chocolate hearts and colorful heart candies.

President's Day Board

Cheeses:
1.5 oz of each cheese per person
Harvest Moon
Lincolnshire Pocher
Manchego
Zimbro

Meats:
1.5 oz per meat per person
Chorizo (sliced)
Serrano Ham (thinly sliced and rolled up)
Sopressata (sliced)

Wine Suggestions:
Cava and Rioja (red) pair well with all cheeses and meats

Accompaniments:
Ciabatta bread (sliced), star shaped crackers, water crackers, olive tapenade, honey and/or honeycomb, figs (quartered), strawberries, blueberries, red seedless grapes, dried apricots, almonds, cashews and cornishons.

St. Patrick's Day Board

Cheeses:
1.5 oz of each cheese per person
Durrus
Gubbeen
Milleens

Meats:
1.5 oz per meat per person
Corned beef (thinly sliced)
Irish Bangers (sliced)

Wine Suggestions:
Sparkling Wine (white), Gewüztraminer and Irish Porter Beer pair well with all cheeses and meats

Accompaniments:
Soda bread and Irish potato bread (sliced thin), water crackers, scotch eggs, green olives, Dijon mustard, fig jam, walnuts, hazelnuts, dried apricots and gherkins. Decorate with green wrapped chocolate shamrocks.

Easter Board

Cheeses:
1.5 oz of each cheese per person
Appleby's Cheshire
Cheddar, Smoked
Elk Mountain
Thomasville Tomme

Meats:
1.5 oz per meat per person
Capicola (rolled up)
Genoa Salami (sliced)
Prosciutto di Parma (rolled up)

Wine Suggestions:
Shiraz, Sparkling Wine (white) or Prosecco (rosé) pair well with all cheeses and meat

Accompaniments:
Bruschetta toasts, crackers in different shapes and textures, cheese twists, deviled eggs, black olives, apricot jam and pecans. Decorate with bunny crackers, red seedless grapes, mini carrots, sliced cucumbers, Cadbury mini chocolate eggs and pomegranates (halved).

Cinco de Mayo Board

Cheeses:
1.5 oz of each cheese per person
Adobera
Cotija
Queso Blanco

Wine Suggestions:
Cava pairs well with all cheeses
Chardonnay pairs well with Adobera and Queso Blanco
Cabernet Sauvignon and Mezcal pair well with Cotija

Accompaniments:
Corn tortilla chips, guacamole, beef empanadas, nachos, sliced chorizo, pico de gallo, sliced bolillo bread, Serrano ham and pimento stuffed olives. Decorate with fresh cilantro, sliced limes, mini bell peppers and sliced cucumbers.

Mother's Day Board

Cheese:
1.5 oz of each cheese per person
Camembert
Chèvre
Cremont
Pleasant Ridge Reserve

Meats:
1.5 oz of each meat per person
Genoa Salami
Prosciutto di Parma (rolled up)

Wine Suggestions:
Champagne or Sparkling Wine (white) pair well with all cheeses and meat

Accompaniments:
Baguette (sliced thin), water crackers, heart shaped crackers, pâté de foie gras, green olives, strawberries, raspberries, figs (quartered), white seedless grapes, almonds, pecans, fig jam and honeycomb. Decorate with small colorful flowers.

Memorial Day Board

Cheese:
1.5 oz of each cheese per person
Marco Polo
Mimolette
Pecorino
Purple Moon Cheddar

Meats:
1.5 oz of each meat per person
Genoa Salami
Saucisson Sec (sliced thin)

Wine Suggestions:
Bordeaux (red), Cabernet Sauvignon and Sparkling Wine (rosé) pair well with all cheeses and meats

Accompaniments:
French baguette (sliced thin), water crackers, Triscuits, heart shaped crackers, truffle mousse pâté, cornishons, dried apricots, walnuts, pistachios, green and black olives, blueberries, strawberries, pomegranates (halved). Decorate with mozzarella stars (use a cookie cutter).

Father's Day Board

Cheese:
1.5 oz of each cheese per person
Ascutney Mountain
Calvander
Crowley
Parmigiano Reggiano

Meats:
1.5 oz of each meat per person
Chorizo (sliced)
Coppa
Rosbife (sliced thin)
Serrano Ham

Wine Suggestions:
Cabernet Sauvignon and Sparkling Wine (rosé or white) pair well with all cheeses and meats

Accompaniments:
Baguette (sliced thin), water crackers, multigrain crackers, olive tapenade, gherkins, walnuts, pistachios, dried apricots, carrots and celery sticks, red seedless grapes and apple chutney. Garnish with rosemary springs and cheery tomatoes.

Labor Day Board

Cheese:
1.5 oz of each cheese per person
Appalachian
Challerhocker
Gouda
Trillium

Meats:
1.5 oz of each meat per person
Coppa
Saucisson Sec
Serrano Ham

Wine Suggestions:
Chardonnay and Sparkling Wine (white) pair well with all cheeses and meats

Accompaniments:
French baguette (sliced thin), crostini, flatbread crackers, wheat rounds, watermelon triangles, blueberries, cherries, red seedless grapes, strawberries, blue cheese dip, celery and carrot sticks, radishes and cucumber slices. Garnish with star shaped mozzarella cheese.

Halloween Board

Cheese:
1.5 oz of each cheese per person
Cheddar
Five Counties
Purple Moon Cheedar
Roaring Forties Blue

Meats:
1.5 oz of each meat per person
Bresaola (sliced thin)
Mortadella (sliced thin)
Rosbeef (sliced thin)

Wine Suggestions:
Cabernet Sauvignon and Sparkling Wine (rosé or white) pair well with all cheeses and meat

Accompaniments:
French baguette (sliced thin), water crackers, bruschetas, baba ganousch, honey or honeycomb, beet chips, purple cauliflower, blackberries, red seedless grapes, persimmons, almonds, pimento stuffed green olives and conrnichons. Garnish with candy corn, mini pumpkins and small black plastic spiders.

Thanksgiving Board

Cheeses:
1.5 oz of each cheese per person
Gruyére
Robiola Bosina
Rogue River Blue
Tallegio

Meats:
1.5 oz of each meat per person
Serrano Ham
Genoa Salami

Wine Suggestions:
Champagne, Sparkling Wine (white), Cava or Franciacorta pair well with all cheeses and meats

Accompaniments:
Thanksgiving dinner is very filling. This board does not have many accompaniments to save space for the dinner. French baguette (sliced thin), water crackers, cheese straws, cornishons and green olives. Decorate with figs (halved), mini pumpkins, persimmons, dried orange slices and maple leaf cookies.

Christmas Board

Cheese:
1.5 oz of each cheese per person
Bleu d'Auvergne
Chévre
Havarti
Manchego

Meats:
1.5 oz per meat per person
Genoa Salami
Prosciutto di Parma
Sopressata (sliced thin)

Wine Suggestions:
Champagne, Sparkling Wine (white), Cava or Franciacorta pair well with all cheeses and meats

Accompaniments:
French baguette (sliced thin), star shaped and Christmas tree shaped crackers, ciabatta bread (sliced thin), pistachios, almonds, green and black olives, dried cranberries, strawberries, green and red seedless grapes, quince paste and dried apricots. Decorate with cherry tomatoes and rosemary springs.

INDIVIDUAL PLATES

If instead of a cheese board you would like to serve individual plates before or after dinner – as they do in France, for exemple – you can serve one, two or three pieces of cheese. Serve them in small slices with one accompaniment or garnish. Some suggestions:

- Camembert, Sliced Apples and Chardonnay

- Chaource, Red Seedless Grapes and Champagne

- Chèvre, Strawberries and Champagne

- Comté, Walnuts and Vin Jeune di Savoie

- Crottin de Chavignol, Sliced Peaches and Sancerre

- Époisses, Thin Baguette Slices and Gevrey-Chambertin

- Gorgonzola, Figs and Vin Santo

- Manchego, Jamon Ibérico and Amontillado Sherry

- Parmigiano Reggiano, Balsamic Vinegar and Chianti Classico

- Pecorino, Olive Oil and Chianti Classico

COUNTRY WINE LIST

Sparkling Wine

Cava – Spain

Champagne – France

Crémant d'Alsace – France

Crémant de Loire – France

Crémant du Jura – France

Sparkling Wine (white) – Any Country

Sparkling Wine (rosé) – Any Country

Franciacorta – Italy

Lambrusco – Italy

Lambrusco di Sobarba – Italy

Prosecco – Italy

Sekt – Germany

White Wine

Airén – Spain

Albariño – Spain

Albillo – Spain

Alvarinho – Portugal

Anjou – France

Arbois – France

Assyrtico – Greece

Beaujolais – France

Bourdeaux – France

Burgundy – France

Chablis – France

Chardonnay – Any Country

Chasselas – France

Chateauneuf-du-Pape – France

Chenin Blanc – France

Côtes-du-Rhône – France

Crozes-Hermitage – France

Dão – Portugal

Entre-Deux-Mers – France

Faugères – France

Fiano di Avellino – Italy

Fumé Blanc – United States

Gave – Italy

Gewürztraminer – Germany, Alsace (France)

Grechetto – Italy

Greco di Tufo – Italy

Grenache Blanc – France

Grüner Veltliner – Áustria

Jura – France

Jurançon – France

Loire – France

Malvasia – Italy

Moscato – Italy

Müller-Thurgau – Germany

Muscadet – France
Orvieto – Italy
Pecorino – Italy
Pessac-Léognan – France
Pinot Blanc – France
Pinot Gris – France
Pinot Meunier – France
Pouilly-Fumé – France
Ribeiro – Spain
Ribera del Guadiana – Spain
Riesling – Germany
Rioja – Spain
Robola – Greece
Roditis – Greece
Roero Arneis –Italy
Roussanne – France
Sancerre – France
Sauvignon Blanc – Any Country
Savagnin – France
Schiava – Italy
Sémillon – France
Seyssel – France
Soave – Italy
Torrontés – Argentine
Trebbiano – Italy
Verdejo – Spain

Vermentino – Italy
Vernaccia di San Gimignano di San Gimignano – Italy
Vidal Blanc – Canadá, United States
Vidiano – Greece
Vinho Verde (white) – Portugal
Viognier – France
Vouvray – France
Zinfandel – United States

Rosé Wine

Côtes-du-Rhône – France
Garnacha – Spain
Grenache – Any Country
Loire - France
Malbec – Argentine
Pinot Noir – Any Country
Provence – France
Shiraz – United States
Syrah – Any Country

Red Wine

Agiorgitiko – Greece
Aglianico – Australia, California and Italy
Aglianico del Vulture – Italy
Amarone della Valpolicella– Italy
Barbaresco – Italy

Barbera d'Alba – Italy
Bardolino – Italy
Barolo – Italy
Beaujolais – France
Beaujolais Village – France
Blaüfrankish – Germany
Bobal – Spain
Bonarda – Italy, Argentine
Burgundy – France
Bourdeaux – France
Brunello di Montalcino – Italy
Cabernet Franc – Any Country
Cabernet Sauvignon – Any Country
Cahors – France
Cannonau – Italy
Carignan – France
Carménère – Any Country
Castelão – Portugal
Chambourcin – France
Chianti – Italy
Chinon – France
Colli di Luno Rosso – Italy
Corbières – France
Côtes de Nuit – France
Dolcetto – Italy
Gamay – France

Garnacha – Spain

Graves – France

Grenache – France

Lagrein – Italy

La Mancha – Spain

Lambrusco – Italy

Madiran – France

Malbec – Argentine

Mencia – Spain

Merlot – Any Country

Minervois – France

Monastrell – Spain

Monica di Sardegna – Italy

Montepulciano d'Abruzzo – Italy

Moschofilero – Greece

Murcia – Spain

Navarra – Spain

Nebbiolo – Italy

Nero d'Avola – Italy

Pelješac – Croatia

Pinot Nero – Italy

Pinot Noir – Any Country

Pomerol – France

Poulsard – France

Primitivo – Italy

Priorat – Spain

Raboso Piave – Italy
Reccioto della Valpolicella – Italy
Ribera del Duero – Spain
Rioja – Spain
Rioja Crianza – Spain
Rioja Joven – Spain
Rondo – Germany
Sagrantino di Montefalco – Italy
Saint-Chinian – France
Saint-Émillion – France
Sangiovese – Italy
Shiraz – Australia, United States
Syrah – Any Country
Taurasi Riserva – Italy
Tempranillo – Spain
Touraine – France
Valpolicella – Italy
Valpolicella Ripasso – Italy
Velletri – Italy
Xinomavro – Greece
Zinfandel – United States
Zweigelt – Austria

Dessert Wine

Bonnezeaux – France
Fior d'Arancio – Italy

Late Harvest Chenin Blanc – Any Country
Late Harvest Madeleine Angevine – United States
Icewine – Germany, Canadá
Juraçon Moelleux – France
Monbazillac – France
Moscato d'Asti – Italy
Riesling Auslese – Germany
Riesling Spätlese – Germany
Sauternes – France
Sylvaner Spätlese – Germany
Tokaji – Italy
Vin Santo – Italy

Fortified Wine

Amontillado Sherry – Spain
Banyuls – France
Fino Sherry – Spain
LBV Port – Portugal
Malmsey Madeira – Madeira Island
Manzanilla Sherry – Spain
Maury – France
Oloroso Sherry – Spain
Palo Cortado Sherry – Spain
Pineau des Charentes – France
Sercial Madeira – Madeira Island
Tawny Port – Portugal

Tawny Port 10 Years Old – Portugal
Vintage Port – Portugal
White Port – Portugal

Other Drinks

Aquavit –Scandinavia
Cognac – France
Irish Porter Beer – Ireland
Mezcal – Mexico

BIBLIOGRAPHY

Beckett, Fiona, *101 Great Ways to Enjoy Cheese & Wine*, E-book, 2017

Beckett, Fiona, *101 Great Ways to Enjoy Sherry*, E-book, 2017

Cabral, Bruno, *Queijos Brasileiros à Mesa com Cachaça, Vinho e Cerveja*, Editora Senac São Paulo, 2017

Centamore, Adam, *Tasting Wine and Cheese*, Quarry Books, 2015

Dowey, Mary *Food and Wine Pairing Made Simple*, Ryland, Peters & Small, 2002

Fletcher, Janet, *Cheese and Wine*, Chronicle Books, 2007

Goldstein, Evan and Joyce, *Perfect Pairings: A Master Sommelier's Practical Advice for Partnering Wine and Food*, University of California Press, 2006

Harrington, Robert J., *Food and Wine Pairing: A Sensory Experience*, Wiley, 2007

Jones, Steve, *Cheese, Beer, Wine, Cider: A Field Guide* to *75 Perfect Pairings*, Countryman Press, 2019

Keenan, Tia, *The Art of the Cheese Platter*, Rizzoli, 2006

Laloganes, John Peter, *The Essentials of Wine and Food Pairing Techniques*, Pearson, 2009

Macneil, Karen, *Wine, Food and Friends*, Oxmoor House, 2006

McCarthy, Ed, *Wine for Dummies*, Wiley Publishing, 2018

Muir, Roberta, *500 Cheeses*, Sellers Publishing, Inc., 2003

Werlin, Laura, *The All American Cheese and Wine Book*, Haary N. Abrahams, 2003

CHEESE, MEAT AND ACCOMPANIMENTS SOURCES

www.beechershandmadecheese.com
www.blackberryfarm.com
www.cowgirlcreamery.com
www.gourmet-food.com/cheese
www.igourmet.com
www.supermarketitaly.com
www.cheesemongershop.com
www.cheesemonthclub.com
www.murray'scheese.com
www.caputos.com
www.roguecreamery.com
www.saxelbycheesemongers.com
www.williamsonoma.com
www.wisconsincheese.com

WEBSITES

www.cheese.com
www.cheesemag.com
www.foodandwine.com
www.jancisrobinson.com
www.matchingfoodandwine.com
www.platsetvins.fr

www.thewinesociety.com
www.winefolly.com
www.winespectator.com
www.wineenthusiast.com

ABOUT THE AUTHOR

Leonardo Linosk author of *Which Wine? 1900 Food and Wine Pairings* is a Fisar (Federazione Italiana Sommelier Albergatori e Ristoratorie) Professional Sommelier since 2009 and took innumerous wine courses throughout the world. Food and wine pairing is his passion. Leonardo lives in Bend, Oregon.

Printed in Great Britain
by Amazon

10037341R00099